HEALTHY CHOICES

FOR WOMEN

100 Days of Devotions

For
Mind,
Body,
and Spirit

The quoted ideas expressed in this book (but not Scripture verses) are not, in all cases, exact quotations, as some have been edited for clarity and brevity. In all cases, the author has attempted to maintain the speaker's original intent. In some cases, quoted material for this book was obtained from secondary sources, primarily print media. While every effort was made to ensure the accuracy of these sources, the accuracy cannot be guaranteed. For additions, deletions, corrections, or clarifications in future editions of this text, please write Freeman-Smith, LLC.

The Holy Bible, King James Version

The Holy Bible, New King James Version (NKJV) Copyright © 1982 by Thomas Nelson, Inc. Used by permission.

New Century Version®. (NCV) Copyright © 1987, 1988, 1991 by Word Publishing, a division of Thomas Nelson, Inc. All rights reserved. Used by permission.

The Holman Christian Standard Bible™ (HCSB) Copyright © 1999, 2000, 2001 by Holman Bible Publishers. Used by permission.

The Holy Bible, New International Version®. (NIV) Copyright © 1973, 1978, 1984 International Bible Society. Used by permission of Zondervan. All rights reserved.

The Holy Bible. New Living Translation (NLT) copyright © 1996 Tyndale Charitable Trust. Used by permission of Tyndale House Publishers.

The New American Standard Bible®, (NASB) Copyright © 1960, 1962, 1963, 1968, 1971, 1972, 1973, 1975, 1977, 1995 by The Lockman Foundation. Used by permission.

Scripture taken from The Message. (MSG) Copyright © 1993, 1994, 1995, 1996, 2000, 2001, 2002. Used by permission of NavPress Publishing Group.

Cover Design by Kim Russell / Wahoo Designs
Page Layout by Bart Dawson

ISBN 978-1-60587-273-5

HEALTHY CHOICES

CHOICES

FOR WOMEN

100 Days of Devotions

For
Mind,
Body,
and Spirit

A MESSAGE TO READERS

A wise man will hear and increase learning, and a man of understanding will attain wise counsel.

Proverbs 1:5 NKJV

The advice in this book is general in nature, and your circumstances are specific to you. For that reason, we strongly suggest that you consult your physician before beginning any new regimen of physical exercise or diet. Don't depend upon this book—or any other book like it—to be your sole source of information on matters pertaining to your health. Instead, consider Proverbs 1:5 and seek wise counsel from a variety of sources, especially your personal physician, before making major health-related decisions.

INTRODUCTION

Countless books have been written on the topics of health and fitness. But if you're a Christian, you probably already own at least one copy—and more likely several copies—of the world's foremost guide to spiritual, physical, and emotional fitness. That book is the Holy Bible. The Bible is the irreplaceable guidebook for faithful believers—like you—who seek God's wisdom and His truth.

God has a plan for every aspect of your life, including your food, your fitness, and your faith. But God will not force His plans upon you; to the contrary, He has given you the ability to make choices. The consequences of those choices help determine·the quality and the tone of your life. This book is intended to help you make wise choices—choices that will lead to spiritual, physical, and emotional health—by encouraging you to rely heavily upon the promises of God's Holy Word.

Health is a gift from God. What we do with that gift is determined, to a surprising extent, by the person we see every time we gaze into the mirror. If we squander our health—or if we take it for granted—we do a profound disservice to ourselves and to our loved ones. But God has other plans. He commands us to treat our bodies, our minds, and our souls with the utmost care. And that's exactly what we should do.

If you seek to protect and to enhance your spiritual, emotional, and physical health, these pages will help, but they offer no shortcuts. Healthy living is a journey, not a destination, and that journey requires discipline. If you're willing to make the step-by-step journey toward improved health, rest assured that God is taking careful note of your progress . . . and He's quietly urging you to take the next step.

DAY 1

100 DAYS TO A NEW AND IMPROVED YOU

A prudent person foresees the danger ahead and takes precautions. The simpleton goes blindly on and suffers the consequences.

Proverbs 27:12 NLT

It takes time to change a habit, but it doesn't take forever. In fact, if you can do anything for 100 straight days, then there's a very good chance you can keep doing it on the 101st, the 102nd, and beyond. If you thought that you could establish a number of healthy habits, would you be willing to carve out a few minutes each day for the next few months in order to find out? If you answered yes, congratulations. You're about to embark on a grand adventure.

> When you form a deeper relationship with God, you can start establishing healthier habits, starting now.

This book contains 100 chapters, each of which contains a devotional message about your mind, your body, and your spirit. If you read each devotional carefully—and if you implement the ideas that you find there—you can have a profound impact on your own life and upon the lives of your loved ones.

FOOD FOR THOUGHT

You can build up a set of good habits so that you habitually take the Christian way without thought.

E. Stanley Jones

You will never change your life until you change something you do daily.

John Maxwell

If you want to form a new habit, get to work. If you want to break a bad habit, get on your knees.

Marie T. Freeman

Do you not know that your body is a sanctuary of the Holy Spirit who is in you, whom you have from God? You are not your own, for you were bought at a price; therefore glorify God in your body.

1 Corinthians 6:19-20 HCSB

A HEALTHY-CHOICE TIP

Before you begin a major new exercise program, see your doctor: As the old saying goes, it's better to be safe than sorry.

FORMING HEALTHY HABITS

Dear friend, I pray that you may prosper in every way and be in good health, just as your soul prospers.

3 John 1:2 HCSB

First, you make your habits, and then your habits make you. Some habits will inevitably bring you closer to God; other habits will lead you away from the path He has chosen for you. If you sincerely desire to improve your spiritual health, you must honestly examine the habits that make up the fabric of your day. And you must abandon those habits that are displeasing to God.

Today, ask God to help you form healthier habits. If you ask for His help—if you petition Him sincerely and often—your Heavenly Father will guide your steps and protect you from harmful behaviors.

If you trust God, and if you keep asking for His help, He can transform your life. If you sincerely ask Him to help you, the same God who created the universe will help you defeat the harmful habits that have heretofore defeated you. So, if at first you don't succeed, keep praying. God is listening, and He's ready to help you become a better person if you ask Him . . . so ask today.

FOOD FOR THOUGHT

We are never out of reach of Satan's devices, so we must never be without the whole armor of God.

Warren Wiersbe

Begin to be now what you will be hereafter.

St. Jerome

Acquire wisdom—how much better it is than gold! And acquire understanding—it is preferable to silver.

Proverbs 16:16 HCSB

A HEALTHY-CHOICE TIP

Do you dine out often? If so, be careful. Most restaurants stay in business by serving big portions of tasty food. Unfortunately, most restaurant food is high in calories, sugar, and fat. You will probably eat healthier meals if you prepare those meals at home instead of eating out.

RESPECTING YOUR BODY

Therefore, brothers, by the mercies of God, I urge you to present your bodies as a living sacrifice, holy and pleasing to God; this is your spiritual worship.

Romans 12:1 HCSB

In the 12th chapter of Romans, Paul encourages us to take special care of the bodies God has given us. But it's tempting to do otherwise.

We live in a fast-food world where unhealthy choices are convenient, inexpensive, and tempting. And, we live in a digital world filled with modern conveniences that often rob us of the physical exercise needed to maintain healthy lifestyles. As a result, too many of us find ourselves glued to the television, with a snack in one hand and a clicker in the other. The results are as unfortunate as they are predictable.

> If you're not determined to be the master of your body . . . then you might just become a slave to your impulses.

God's Word teaches us that our bodies are "temples" which belong to God (1 Corinthians 6:19-20). We are commanded (not encouraged, not advised—we are commanded!) to treat our bodies with respect and honor. We do so by making wise choices and by making those choices consistently: day by day, month by month, and year by year.

FOOD FOR THOUGHT

Eat to live, and not live to eat.

Poor Richard's Almanac

Our body is like armor, our soul like the warrior. Take care of both, and you will be ready for what comes.

Amma St. Syncletice

For it was You who created my inward parts; You knit me together in my mother's womb. I will praise You, because I have been remarkably and wonderfully made.

Psalm 139:13-14 HCSB

A HEALTHY-CHOICE TIP

Take a few minutes to examine your eating habits. Do you gobble down snack foods while watching television? If so, stop. Do you drink high-calorie soft drinks or feast on unhealthy snacks like potato chips or candy? If so, you're doing yourself a disservice. Do you load up your plate and then feel obligated to eat every last bite? If so, it's time to form some new habits.

Poor eating habits are usually well established, so they won't be easy to change, but change them you must if you want to enjoy the benefits of a healthy lifestyle.

DAY 4

FAITH AND FITNESS

Cast your burden on the Lord, and He shall sustain you; He shall never permit the righteous to be moved.

Psalm 55:22 NKJV

Faith and fitness. These two words may seem disconnected, but they are not. If you're about to begin a regimen of vigorous physical exercise, then you will find it helpful to begin a regimen of vigorous spiritual exercise, too. Why? Because the physical, emotional, and spiritual aspects of your life are interconnected. In other words, you cannot "compartmentalize" physical fitness in one category of your being and spiritual fitness in another—every facet of your life has an impact on the person you are today and the person you will become tomorrow. That's why your body is so important to God—your body is, quite literally, the "temple" that houses "the Spirit of God" that dwells within you (1 Corinthians 3:16).

Today, spend time thinking about God's plans for your spiritual and physical health.

God's Word contains powerful lessons about every aspect of your life, including your health. So, if you're concerned about your spiritual, physical, or emotional health, the first place to turn is that timeless source of comfort and assurance, the Holy Bible. When you open your Bible and begin reading, you'll quickly be reminded of this fact:

when you face concerns of any sort—including health-related challenges—God is with you. And His healing touch, like His love, endures forever.

FOOD FOR THOUGHT

The Christian faith is meant to be lived moment by moment. It isn't some broad, general outline—it's a long walk with a real Person. Details count: passing thoughts, small sacrifices, a few encouraging words, little acts of kindness, brief victories over nagging sins.

Joni Eareckson Tada

Only by walking with God can we hope to find the path that leads to life.

John Eldredge

STRENGTHENING YOUR FAITH

God has given us the Bible for the purpose of knowing His promises, His power, His commandments, His wisdom, His love, and His Son. As we study God's teachings and apply them to our lives, we live by the Word that shall never pass away. So if you're about to begin a new fitness program, be sure that you also pay careful attention to God's program by studying His Word every day of your life.

DON'T GO ON A DIET, CHANGE YOUR LIFESTYLE

Their end is destruction; their god is their stomach; their glory is in their shame. They are focused on earthly things.

Philippians 3:19 HCSB

If you want to lose weight, don't dare go on a diet! It's a sad fact, but true: in the vast majority of cases, diets simply don't work. In fact, one study that examined the results of popular diets conducted that nearly 100% of dieters suffered almost "complete relapse after 3 to 5 years." In other words, dieters almost always return to their pre-diet weights (or, in many cases, to even higher weight levels).

If diets don't work, what should you do if you weigh more than you should? The answer is straightforward: If you need to lose weight, don't start dieting; change your lifestyle.

> It takes wisdom to be moderate; moderation is wisdom in action.

Your current weight is the result of the number of calories that you have taken into your body versus the number of calories that you have burned. If you seek to lower your weight, then you must burn more calories (by engaging in more vigorous physical activities), or take in fewer calories (by eating more sensibly), or both. It's as simple as that.

FOOD FOR THOUGHT

It's not that some people have willpower and some don't. It's that some people are ready to change and others are not.

James Gordon, M.D.

We are all created differently. We share a common need to balance the different parts of our lives.

Dr. Walt Larimore

You can look at your calorie count in the same way you might look at a bank account. Every mouthful of food is a deposit and every activity that requires energy is a withdrawal. If we deposit more then we withdraw, our surplus grows larger and larger.

John Maxwell

To many, total abstinence is easier than perfect moderation.

St. Augustine

A HEALTHY-CHOICE TIP

Are you skipping meals? Don't do it. Skipping meals isn't healthy, and it isn't a sensible way to lose weight, either.

DAY 6

SAY NO TO
UNHEALTHY FOODS

*Don't you know that you are God's sanctuary and that the
Spirit of God lives in you?*

1 Corinthians 3:16 HCSB

Eating unhealthy foods is habit-forming. And if you have
acquired the unfortunate habit of eating unhealthy foods,
then God wants you start to making changes today.

Take a few more minutes than you did on day 3 to
think about your eating habits. Are you really ready to improve your diet, your health, and your life?

Poor eating habits are easy to make and hard to break,
but break them you must. Otherwise, you'll be disobeying God's commandments while causing
yourself great harm.

Think about ways
that your spiritual
health impacts your
physical health, and
vice-versa.

Maintaining a healthy lifestyle is
a journey, not a destination, and that
journey requires discipline. But rest assured that if you and your loved ones are
willing to make the step-by-step journey
toward a healthier diet, God is taking careful note of your
progress . . . and He's quietly urging you to take the next
step.

FOOD FOR THOUGHT

Food ought to be a refreshment to the body, and not a burden.

St. Bonaventure

The key to healthy eating is moderation and managing what you eat every day.

John Maxwell

In general, mankind, since the improvement of cookery, eats twice as much as nature requires.

Ben Franklin

A HEALTHY-CHOICE TIP

Adopt healthy habits you can stick with. In other words, don't starve yourself. And if you're beginning an exercise regimen, start slowly. Be moderate, even in your moderation.

PUT GOD IN HIS RIGHTFUL PLACE

Do not have other gods besides Me.

Exodus 20:3 HCSB

As you think about the nature of your relationship with God, remember this: you will always have some type of relationship with Him—it is inevitable that your life must be lived in relationship to God. The question is not if you will have a relationship with Him; the burning question is whether that relationship will be one that seeks to honor Him . . . or not.

Are you willing to place God first in your life? And, are you willing to welcome Him into your heart? Unless you can honestly answer these questions with a resounding yes, then your relationship with God isn't what it could be or should be. Thankfully, God is always available, He's always ready to forgive, and He's waiting to hear from you now. The rest, of course, is up to you.

You must guard your heart by putting God in His rightful place—first place.

FOOD FOR THOUGHT

It is when we come to the Lord in our nothingness, our powerlessness and our helplessness that He then enables us to love in a way which, without Him, would be absolutely impossible.

Elisabeth Elliot

When all else is gone, God is still left. Nothing changes Him.

Hannah Whitall Smith

If God has the power to create and sustain the universe, He is more than able to sustain your marriage and your ministry, your faith and your finances, your hope and your health.

Anne Graham Lotz

Love has its source in God, for love is the very essence of His being.

Kay Arthur

STRENGTHENING YOUR FAITH

As you establish priorities for your day and your life, God deserves first place. And you deserve the experience of putting Him there.

SO MANY TEMPTATIONS

The LORD is my strength and song, and He has become my salvation; He is my God, and I will praise Him…

Exodus 15:2 NKJV

Our world is teeming with temptations and distractions that can rob you of the physical, emotional, and spiritual fitness that might otherwise be yours. And if you're not careful, the struggles and stresses of everyday living can rob you of the peace that should rightfully be yours because of your personal relationship with Christ. So take time each day to have a personal training session with your Savior.

Today, think about the ways that your spiritual, emotional, and physical health are interconnected.

Don't be a woman who's satisfied with occasional visits to church on Sunday morning; build a relationship with Jesus that deepens day by day. When you do, you will most certainly encounter the subtle hand of the Father. Then, if you are wise, you will take His hand and follow God as He leads you on the path to a healthier, happier life.

FOOD FOR THOUGHT

Measure the size of the obstacles against the size of God.

Beth Moore

God wants to reveal Himself as your Heavenly Father. When you wonder which way to turn, you can grasp His strong hand, and He'll guide you along life's path.

Lisa Whelchel

Do not fight the temptation in detail. Turn from it. Look ONLY at your Lord. Sing. Read. Work.

Amy Carmichael

Temptation is not a sin. Even Jesus was tempted. The Lord Jesus gives you the strength needed to resist temptation.

Corrie ten Boom

A HEALTHY-CHOICE TIP

If life's inevitable temptations seem to be getting the best of you, try praying more often, even if many of those prayers are simply brief, "open-eyed" requests to your Father in heaven.

HAVE A REGULAR APPOINTMENT WITH GOD

But have nothing to do with irreverent and silly myths. Rather, train yourself in godliness.

1 Timothy 4:7 HCSB

Each new day is a gift from God, and if we are wise, we spend a few quiet moments each morning thanking the Giver. Daily life is woven together with the threads of habit, and no habit is more important to our spiritual health than the discipline of daily prayer and devotion to the Creator.

When we begin each day with heads bowed and hearts lifted, we remind ourselves of God's love, His protection, and His commandments. And if we are wise, we align our priorities for the coming day with the teachings and commandments that God has given us through His Holy Word.

> You need a regular appointment with your Creator. God is ready to talk to you, and you should prepare yourself each morning to talk to Him.

Are you seeking to change some aspect of your life? Do you seek to improve the condition of your spiritual or physical health? If so, ask for God's help and ask for it many times each day . . . starting with your morning devotional.

FOOD FOR THOUGHT

I suggest you discipline yourself to spend time daily in a systematic reading of God's Word. Make this "quiet time" a priority that nobody can change.

Warren Wiersbe

We are meddling with God's business when we let all manner of imaginings loose, predicting disaster, contemplating possibilities instead of following, one day at a time, God's plain and simple pathway.

Elisabeth Elliot

Jesus challenges you and me to keep our focus daily on the cross of His will if we want to be His disciples.

Anne Graham Lotz

STRENGTHENING YOUR FAITH

Make a promise to yourself and keep it that you will begin each day with a morning devotional. A regular time of quiet reflection and prayer will allow you to praise your Creator and to focus your thoughts. A daily devotional is especially important during those times of your life when you're feeling discouraged or fearful.

IF NOT NOW, WHEN?

Therefore, get your minds ready for action, being self-disciplined, and set your hope completely on the grace to be brought to you at the revelation of Jesus Christ.

1 Peter 1:13 HCSB

If you're determined to improve the state of your physical, spiritual, or emotional health, the best time to begin is now. But if you're like most people, you'll be tempted to put things off until tomorrow, or the next day, or the next.

The habit of putting things off until the last minute, along with its first cousin, the habit of making excuses for work that was never done, can be detrimental to your life, to your character, and to your health. Are you in the habit of doing what needs to be done when it needs to be done, or are you a dues-paying member of the Procrastinator's Club? If you're a woman who has already acquired the habit of doing things sooner rather than later, congratulations! But, if you find yourself putting off all those unpleasant tasks until later (or never), it's time to think about the consequences of your behavior.

When it comes to food, fitness, or faith, the best moment to begin major improvements is the present moment.

One way that you can learn to defeat procrastination is by paying less attention to the sacrifices you're making today and more attention to the rewards you'll receive to-morrow. So, if you're trying to improve your fitness, or any other aspect of your life, don't spend endless hours fretting over your fate. Simply seek God's counsel and get busy. When you do, you will be richly rewarded because of your willingness to act.

FOOD FOR THOUGHT

We spend our lives dreaming of the future, not realizing that a little of it slips away every day.

Barbara Johnson

Do noble things, do not dream them all day long.

Charles Kingsley

A HEALTHY-CHOICE TIP

Healthy choices are easy to put off until some future date. But procrastination, especially concerning matters of personal health, is, at best, foolish and, at worst, dangerous. If you feel the need to improve your physical health, don't wait for New Year's Day; don't even wait until tomorrow. The time to begin living a healthier life is the moment you finish reading this sentence.

DAY 11

TRUSTING GOD AND FINDING BALANCE

Don't burn out; keep yourselves fueled and aflame. Be alert servants of the Master, cheerfully expectant. Don't quit in hard times; pray all the harder.

Romans 12:11-12 MSG

Face facts: life is a delicate balancing act, a tightrope walk with over-commitment on one side and under-commitment on the other. And it's up to each of us to walk carefully on that rope, not falling prey to pride (which causes us to attempt too much) or to fear (which causes us to attempt too little).

God's Word promises us the possibility of abundance (John 10:10). And we are far more likely to experience that abundance when we lead balanced lives.

> A regularly scheduled time of prayer, Bible reading, and meditation can help you prioritize your day and your life.

When you allow yourself to take on too many jobs, you simply can't do all of them well. That means that if you allow yourself to become overcommitted, whether at home, at work, at church, or anywhere in between, you're asking for trouble. So you must learn how to say no to the things you don't have the time or the energy to do.

Of course, sometimes, saying no can be tough. Why? Because well-meaning women (like you) genuinely want to help other people out. But if you allow yourself to become overworked, you may begin over-promising and under-serving—and you'll disappoint just about everybody, including yourself.

Are you and your loved ones doing too much—or too little? If so, it's time to have a little chat with God. And if you listen carefully to His instructions, you will strive to achieve a more balanced life, a life that's right for you and your loved ones. When you do, everybody wins.

FOOD FOR THOUGHT

Let's face it. None of us can do a thousand things to the glory of God. And, in our own vain attempt to do so, we stand the risk of forfeiting a precious thing.

Beth Moore

STRENGTHENING YOUR FAITH

Ruth Bell Graham, wife of evangelist Billy Graham, observed: "The Reference Point for the Christian is the Bible. All values, judgments, and attitudes must be gauged in relationship to this Reference Point." Make certain that you're an avid reader of God's bestseller, and make sure that you keep reading it as long as you live!

DO FIRST THINGS FIRST

Therefore, get your minds ready for action, being self-disciplined . . . .

1 Peter 1:13 HCSB

"First things first." These words are easy to speak but hard to put into practice. For a busy woman living in a demanding world, placing first things first can be difficult indeed. Why? Because so many people are expecting so many things from you!

If you're having trouble prioritizing your day, perhaps you've been trying to organize your life according to your own plans, not God's. A better strategy, of course, is to take your daily obligations and place them in the hands of the One who created you. To do so, you must prioritize your day according to God's commandments, and you must seek His will and His wisdom in all matters. Then, you can face the day with the assurance that the same God who created our universe out of nothingness will help you place first things first in your own life.

> Your Heavenly Father wants you to prioritize your day and your life. And the best place to start is by putting God first.

Do you feel overwhelmed or confused? Turn the concerns of this day over to God—prayerfully, earnestly, and often. Then listen for His answer . . . and trust the answer He gives.

FOOD FOR THOUGHT

Sin is largely a matter of mistaken priorities. Any sin in us that is cherished, hidden, and not confessed will cut the nerve center of our faith.

Catherine Marshall

Have you prayed about your resources lately? Find out how God wants you to use your time and your money. No matter what it costs, forsake all that is not of God.

Kay Arthur

There were endless demands on Jesus' time. Still he was able to make that amazing claim of "completing the work you gave me to do." (John 17:4 NIV)

Elisabeth Elliot

A HEALTHY-CHOICE TIP

If you're trying to reshape your physique or your life, don't try to do it alone. Ask for the support and encouragement of your family members and friends. You'll improve your odds of success if you enlist your own cheering section.

IT ALL STARTS WITH GOD

Now the God of all grace, who called you to His eternal glory in Christ Jesus, will personally restore, establish, strengthen, and support you.

1 Peter 5:10 HCSB

Physical fitness, like every other aspect of your life, begins and ends with God. If you'd like to adopt a healthier life-style, God is willing to help. In fact, if you sincerely wish to create a healthier you—either physically, emotionally or spiritually—God is anxious to be your silent partner in that endeavor, but it's up to you to ask for His help.

When you are tired, fearful, or discouraged, God can restore your physical strength and your emotional health.

The journey toward improved health is not only a common-sense exercise in personal discipline, it is also a spiritual journey ordained by our Creator. God does not intend that we abuse our bodies by giving in to excessive appetites or to slothful behavior. To the contrary, God has instructed us to protect our physical bodies to the greatest extent we can. To do otherwise is to disobey Him.

God has a plan for every facet of your life, and His plan includes provisions for your spiritual, physical, and emotional health. But, He expects you to do your fair share of the work! In a world that is chock-full of tasty temptations, you may find it all too easy to make unhealthy choices. Your challenge, of course, is to resist those unhealthy choices by every means you can, including prayer. And you can be sure that whenever you ask for God's help, He will give it.

FOOD FOR THOUGHT

God uses our most stumbling, faltering faith-steps as the open door to His doing for us "more than we ask or think."

Catherine Marshall

Faith is not merely you holding on to God—it is God holding on to you.

E. Stanley Jones

The love of God is so vast, the power of His touch so invigorating, we could just stay in His presence for hours, soaking up His glory, basking in His blessings.

Debra Evans

STRENGTHENING YOUR FAITH

Whatever your weaknesses, God is stronger. And His strength will help you measure up to His tasks.

THE RIGHT KIND OF EXERCISE FOR YOU

He gives strength to the weary and strengthens the powerless.

Isaiah 40:29 HCSB

If you want to attain and maintain a healthy lifestyle, it's important to engage in a consistent exercise program. Implementing a plan of regular, sensible exercise is one way of ensuring that you've done your part to care for the body that God has given you.

Dr. Kenneth Cooper observed, "Physical activity achieved at any level is an essential ingredient in slowing down the process of aging and turning life into a far more useful, enjoyable— and independent—affair." So what's the right kind of exercise for you? That's a question for you and your doctor. But whether you're running marathons or walking around the block, it's important to stay as active as you can, as long as you can.

Your exercise regimen should be sensible, enjoyable, safe, and consistent.

No one can force you to exercise . . . you'll need to make that decision on your own. And if you genuinely desire to please God, it's a decision that you will make today.

FOOD FOR THOUGHT

People who exercise at least 3 hours a week tend to eat a more balanced and a healthier diet.

Dr. Walt Larimore

Give at least two hours every day to exercise, for health must not be sacrificed to learning. A strong body makes the mind strong.

Thomas Jefferson

It is remarkable how one's wits are sharpened by physical exercise.

Pliny the Younger

An early morning walk is a blessing for the whole day.

Henry David Thoreau

A HEALTHY-CHOICE TIP

The benefits of exercise are both both physical and emotional. But no one can exercise for you; it's up to you to exercise, or not.

FOOD MATTERS

Do not carouse with drunkards and gluttons, for they are on their way to poverty.

Proverbs 23:20-21 NLT

Many of us are remarkably ill-informed and amazingly apathetic about the foods we eat. We feast on high-fat fast foods. We swoon over sweets. We order up—and promptly pack away—prodigious portions. The result is a society in which too many of us become the human equivalents of the portions we purchase: oversized.

A healthier strategy, of course, is to pay more attention to the nutritional properties of our foods and less attention their taste. But for those of us who have become accustomed to large quantities of full-flavored, high-calorie foods, old memories indeed die hard.

Today, think carefully about the quality and the quantity of the foods you eat.

Should we count every calorie that we ingest from now until the day the Good Lord calls us home? Probably not. When we focus too intently upon weight reduction, we may make weight loss even harder to achieve. Instead, we should eliminate from our diets the foods that are obviously bad for us and we should eat more of the foods that are obviously good for us. And of course, we should eat sensible amounts, not prodigious portions.

FOOD FOR THOUGHT

Moderation is better than muscle, self-control better than political power.

Proverbs 16:32 MSG

Now the God of all grace, who called you to His eternal glory in Christ Jesus, will personally restore, establish, strengthen, and support you.

1 Peter 5:10 HCSB

Every achievement worth remembering is stained with the blood of diligence and scarred by the wounds of disappointment.

Charles Swindoll

Failure is the path of least persistence.

Anonymous

A HEALTHY-CHOICE TIP

Since God loves you, and since He wants the very best for you, don't you believe that He also wants you to enjoy a healthy lifestyle? Of course He does. And since a healthy lifestyle is what God wants for you, isn't it what you should want, too?

YOUR PARTNERSHIP WITH GOD

So now we can rejoice in our wonderful new relationship with God—all because of what our Lord Jesus Christ has done for us in making us friends of God.

Romans 5:11 NLT

If you're like most women, you've already tried, perhaps on many occasions, to form healthier habits. You've employed your own willpower in a noble effort to create a new, improved, healthier you. You've probably tried to improve various aspects of your spiritual, physical, or emotional health. Perhaps you've gone on diets, or made New Year's resolutions, or tried the latest self-help fad in an attempt to finally make important changes in your life. And if you're like most women, you've been successful . . . for a while. But eventually, those old familiar habits came creeping back into your life, and the improvements that you had made proved to be temporary. This book is intended to help you build a series of healthy habits for your Christian walk . . . and make those habits stick.

> Your journey toward improved health can be, and should be, a journey that you make with God.

As you read through the pages of this book, you will be asked to depend less upon your own willpower and more upon God's power. For 100 days, you'll be asked to focus on three major areas of your life: mind, body, and spirit. And, of this you can be sure: When you form a working relationship with the Creator, there's no limit to the things that the two of you, working together, can do in just 100 days.

FOOD FOR THOUGHT

Measure the size of the obstacles against the size of God.

Beth Moore

God uses our most stumbling, faltering faith-steps as the open door to His doing for us "more than we ask or think."

Catherine Marshall

A HEALTHY-CHOICE TIP

Perhaps you have tended to divide the concerns of your life into two categories: "spiritual" and "other." If so, it's time to reconsider. God intends you to integrate His commandments into every aspect of your life, and that includes your physical and emotional health, too.

DAY 17

ASKING FOR GOD'S HELP

So I say to you, ask, and it will be given to you; seek, and you will find; knock, and it will be opened to you. For everyone who asks receives, and he who seeks finds, and to him who knocks it will be opened.

Luke 11:9-10 NKJV

Do you genuinely want to strengthen your fitness and your faith? If the answer to that question is yes, then you should set aside ample time each morning to ask for God's help.

Is prayer an integral part of your daily life, or is it a hit-or-miss habit? Do you "pray without ceasing," or is your prayer life an afterthought? Do you regularly pray in the quiet moments of the early morning, or do you bow your head only when others are watching?

Today, make certain that you ask God specifically for the things you need.

As Christians, we are instructed to pray often. But it is important to note that genuine prayer requires much more than bending our knees and closing our eyes. Heartfelt prayer is an attitude of the heart.

If your prayers have become more a matter of habit than a matter of passion, you're robbing yourself of a deeper relationship with God. And how can you rectify that situation? By praying more frequently and more fervently.

When you do, God will shower you with His blessings, His grace, and His love.

FOOD FOR THOUGHT

What God gives in answer to our prayers will always be the thing we most urgently need, and it will always be sufficient.

Elisabeth Elliot

God says we don't need to be anxious about anything; we just need to pray about everything.

Stormie Omartian

Are you weak? Weary? Confused? Troubled? Pressured? How is your relationship with God? Is it held in its place of priority? I believe the greater the pressure, the greater your need for time alone with Him.

Kay Arthur

STRENGTHENING YOUR FAITH

There's no corner of your life that's too unimportant to pray about, so pray about everything.

GUARD YOUR HEART AND MIND

Finally, brethren, whatever things are true, whatever things are noble, whatever things are just, whatever things are pure, whatever things are lovely, whatever things are of good report, if there is any virtue and if there is anything praiseworthy— meditate on these things.

Philippians 4:8 NKJV

You are near and dear to God. He loves you more than you can imagine, and He wants the very best for you. And one more thing: God wants you to guard your heart.

Every day, you are faced with choices . . . more choices than you can count. You can do the right thing, or not. You can be prudent, or not. You can be kind, and generous, and obedient to God. Or not.

Today, think about ways that you can guard your heart from temptation and stress.

Today, the world will offer you countless opportunities to let down your guard and, by doing so, make needless mistakes that may injure you or your loved ones. So be watchful and obedient. Guard your heart by giving it to your Heavenly Father; it is safe with Him.

FOOD FOR THOUGHT

He doesn't need an abundance of words. He doesn't need a dissertation about your life. He just wants your attention. He wants your heart.

Kathy Troccoli

Be sober! Be on the alert! Your adversary the Devil is prowling around like a roaring lion, looking for anyone he can devour.

1 Peter 5:8 HCSB

Becoming pure is a process of spiritual growth, and taking seriously the confession of sin during prayer time moves that process along, causing us to purge our life of practices that displease God.

Elizabeth George

Holiness has never been the driving force of the majority. It is, however, mandatory for anyone who wants to enter the kingdom.

Elisabeth Elliot

STRENGTHENING YOUR FAITH

You should do whatever it takes to guard your heart—and with God's help, you can do it.

MODERATION LEADS TO ABUNDANCE

Don't associate with those who drink too much wine, or with those who gorge themselves on meat. For the drunkard and the glutton will become poor, and grogginess will clothe [them] in rags.

Proverbs 23:20-21 HCSB

If you sincerely seek the abundant life that Christ has promised, you must learn to control your appetites before they control you. Good habits, like bad ones, are habit-forming. The sooner you acquire the habit of moderation, the better your chances for a long, happy, abundant life.

Today, think of at least one step you can take to become a more moderate person.

Are you running short on willpower? If so, perhaps you haven't yet asked God to give you strength. The Bible promises that God offers His power to those righteous men and women who earnestly seek it. If your willpower has failed you on numerous occasions, then it's time to turn your weaknesses over to God. If you've been having trouble standing on your own two feet, perhaps it's time to drop to your knees, in prayer.

FOOD FOR THOUGHT

God wants to revolutionize our lives—by showing us how knowing Him can be the most powerful force to help us become all we want to be.

Bill Hybels

Believe and do what God says. The life-changing consequences will be limitless, and the results will be confidence and peace of mind.

Franklin Graham

Peace, peace to you, and peace to your helpers! For your God helps you.

1 Chronicles 12:18 NKJV

A HEALTHY-CHOICE TIP

Life is a gift—health must be earned. We earn good health by cultivating healthy habits. This is the right time for you to commit yourself to a more sensible lifestyle. So take a close look at your habits: how you eat, how you exercise, and how you think about your health. The only way that you'll revolutionize your physical health is to revolutionize the habits that make up the fabric of your day.

LISTENING TO GOD

The one who is from God listens to God's words. This is why you don't listen, because you are not from God.

John 8:47 HCSB

Sometimes God speaks loudly and clearly. More often, He speaks in a quiet voice—and if you are wise, you will be listening carefully when He does. To do so, you must carve out quiet moments each day to study His Word and sense His direction.

Can you quiet yourself long enough to listen to your conscience? Are you attuned to the subtle guidance of your intuition? Are you willing to pray sincerely and then to wait quietly for God's response? Hopefully so. Usually God refrains from sending His messages on stone tablets or city billboards. More often, He communicates in subtler ways. If you sincerely desire to hear His voice, you must listen carefully, and you must do so in the silent corners of your quiet, willing heart.

Today, find time to be quiet and still. Then, in the silence, listen carefully to your Creator.

FOOD FOR THOUGHT

God is always listening.

Stormie Omartian

The center of power is not to be found in summit meetings or in peace conferences. It is not in Peking or Washington or the United Nations, but rather where a child of God prays in the power of the Spirit for God's will to be done in her life, in her home, and in the world around her.

Ruth Bell Graham

When we come to Jesus stripped of pretensions, with a needy spirit, ready to listen, He meets us at the point of need.

Catherine Marshall

We must leave it to God to answer our prayers in His own wisest way. Sometimes, we are so impatient and think that God does not answer. God always answers! He never fails! Be still. Abide in Him.

Mrs. Charles E. Cowman

STRENGTHENING YOUR FAITH

God is trying to get your attention. Are you listening?

BITTERNESS PUTS DISTANCE BETWEEN YOU AND GOD

Hatred stirs up conflicts, but love covers all offenses.

Proverbs 10:12 HCSB

Are you mired in the quicksand of bitterness or regret? If so, it's time to free yourself from the mire. The world holds few if any rewards for those who remain angrily focused upon the past. Still, the act of forgiveness is difficult for all but the most saintly men and women.

Being frail, fallible, imperfect human beings, most of us are quick to anger, quick to blame, slow to forgive, and even slower to forget. Yet we know that it's best to forgive others, just as we, too, have been forgiven.

> You can never fully enjoy the present if you're bitter about the past. Instead of living in the past, make peace with it . . . and move on.

If there exists even one person—including yourself—against whom you still harbor bitter feelings, it's time to forgive and move on. Bitterness, and regret are not part of God's plan for you, but God won't force you to forgive others. It's a job that only you can finish, and the sooner you finish it, the better.

FOOD FOR THOUGHT

Forgiveness is the key that unlocks the door of resentment and the handcuffs of hate. It is a power that breaks the chains of bitterness and the shackles of selfishness.

Corrie ten Boom

Bitterness is a spiritual cancer, a rapidly growing malignancy that can consume your life. Bitterness cannot be ignored but must be healed at the very core, and only Christ can heal bitterness.

Beth Moore

When you harbor bitterness, happiness will dock elsewhere.

Anonymous

Bitterness is the price we charge ourselves for being unwilling to forgive.

Marie T. Freeman

A HEALTHY-CHOICE TIP

Holding a grudge? Drop it! Remember, holding a grudge is like letting somebody live rent-free in your brain . . . so don't do it!

BE AWARE OF YOUR BLESSINGS

Therefore, get your minds ready for action, being self-disciplined, and set your hope completely on the grace to be brought to you at the revelation of Jesus Christ.

1 Peter 1:13 HCSB

Psalm 145 makes this promise: "The LORD is gracious and compassionate, slow to anger and rich in love. The LORD is good to all; he has compassion on all he has made" (vv. 8-9 NIV). As God's children, we are blessed beyond measure, but sometimes, as busy women in a demanding world, we are slow to count our gifts and even slower to give thanks to the Giver. Our blessings include life and health, family and friends, freedom and possessions— for starters. And, the gifts we receive from God are multiplied when we share them with others. May we always give thanks to God for our blessings, and may we always demonstrate our gratitude by sharing them.

> God blesses us in spite of our lives and not because of our lives.
>
> Max Lucado

FOOD FOR THOUGHT

When you and I are related to Jesus Christ, our strength and wisdom and peace and joy and love and hope may run out, but His life rushes in to keep us filled to the brim. We are showered with blessings, not because of anything we have or have not done, but simply because of Him.

Anne Graham Lotz

There is no secret that can separate you from God's love; there is no secret that can separate you from His blessings; there is no secret that is worth keeping from His grace.

Serita Ann Jakes

Jesus intended for us to be overwhelmed by the blessings of regular days. He said it was the reason he had come: "I am come that they might have life, and that they might have it more abundantly."

Gloria Gaither

STRENGTHENING YOUR FAITH

God gives each of us countless blessings. We, in turn, should give Him our thanks and our praise. So remember: the best moment to give thanks is always the present moment.

PRAY CONSTANTLY ABOUT EVERYTHING, INCLUDING YOUR HEALTH

Rejoice always! Pray constantly. Give thanks in everything, for this is God's will for you in Christ Jesus.

1 Thessalonians 5:16-18 HCSB

Too many of us, even well-intentioned believers, tend to "compartmentalize" our waking hours into a few familiar categories: work, rest, play, family time, and worship. To do so is a mistake. Worship and praise should be woven into the fabric of our lives; prayer should never be relegated to a weekly three-hour visit to church on Sunday morning.

Today, spend time thinking about the power of prayer and the role that prayer plays in your life.

Theologian Wayne Oates once admitted, "Many of my prayers are made with my eyes open. You see, it seems I'm always praying about something, and it's not always convenient—or safe—to close my eyes." Dr. Oates understood that God always hears our prayers and that the relative position of our eyelids is of no concern to Him.

Today, find a little more time to lift your concerns to God in prayer. Pray about everything you can think of, including your spiritual, emotional, and physical health.

FOOD FOR THOUGHT

I am able to do all things through Him who strengthens me.

Philippians 4:13 HCSB

What God gives in answer to our prayers will always be the thing we most urgently need, and it will always be sufficient.

Elisabeth Elliot

Pour out your heart to God and tell Him how you feel. Be real, be honest, and when you get it all out, you'll start to feel the gradual covering of God's comforting presence.

Bill Hybels

And He said to me, "My grace is sufficient for you, for My strength is made perfect in weakness."

2 Corinthians 12:9 NKJV

STRENGTHENING YOUR FAITH

When you've got a choice to make, pray about it—one way to make sure that your heart is in tune with God is to pray often. The more you talk to God, the more He will talk to you.

IT TAKES DISCIPLINE

Apply your heart to discipline and your ears to words of knowledge.

Proverbs 23:12 NASB

Physical fitness requires discipline: the discipline to exercise regularly and the discipline to eat sensibly—it's as simple as that. But here's the catch: understanding the need for discipline is easy, but leading a disciplined life can be hard for most of us. Why? Because it's usually more fun to eat a second piece of cake than it is to jog a second lap around the track. But, as we survey the second helpings that all too often find their way on to our plates, we should consider this: as Christians, we are instructed to lead disciplined lives, and when we behave in undisciplined ways, we are living outside God's will.

Today, think about the costs and the benefits of discipline.

God's Word reminds us again and again that our Creator expects us to be disciplined in our thoughts and disciplined in our actions. God doesn't reward laziness, misbehavior, apathy, or shortsightedness. To the contrary, He expects believers to behave with dignity and self-control.

We live in a world in which leisure is glorified and consumption is commercialized. But God has other plans.

He did not create us for lives of gluttony or sloth; He created us for far greater things.

Life's greatest rewards seldom fall into our laps; to the contrary, our greatest accomplishments usually require lots of work, which is perfectly fine with God. After all, He knows that we're up to the task, and He has big plans for us; may we, as disciplined believers, always be worthy of those plans.

FOOD FOR THOUGHT

Work is doing it. Discipline is doing it every day. Diligence is doing it well every day.

Dave Ramsey

No discipline seems enjoyable at the time, but painful. Later on, however, it yields the fruit of peace and righteousness to those who have been trained by it.

Hebrews 12:11 HCSB

A HEALTHY-CHOICE TIP

Discipline matters. It takes discipline to strengthen your faith; it takes discipline to improve your fitness.

TOO BUSY?

Be careful not to forget the Lord.

Deuteronomy 6:12 HCSB

Has the busy pace of life robbed you of the peace that might otherwise be yours through Jesus Christ? If so, you are simply too busy for your own good. Through His Son Jesus, God offers you a peace that passes human understanding, but He won't force His peace upon you; in order to experience it, you must slow down long enough to sense His presence and His love.

> Frustration is not the will of God. There is time to do anything and everything that God wants us to do.
>
> *Elisabeth Elliot*

Today, as a gift to yourself, to your family, and to the world, slow down and claim the inner peace that is your spiritual birthright: the peace of Jesus Christ. It is offered freely; it has been paid for in full; it is yours for the asking. So ask. And then share.

FOOD FOR THOUGHT

If you can't seem to find time for God, then you're simply too busy for your own good. God is never too busy for you, and you should never be too busy for Him.

Marie T. Freeman

The demand of every day kept me so busy that I subconsciously equated my busyness with commitment to Christ.

Vonette Bright

In our tense, uptight society where folks are rushing to make appointments they have already missed, a good laugh can be as refreshing as a cup of cold water in the desert.

Barbara Johnson

We often become mentally and spiritually barren because we're so busy.

Franklin Graham

STRENGTHENING YOUR FAITH

The world wants to grab every spare minute of your time, but God wants some of your time, too. When in doubt, trust God.

TACKLING TOUGH TIMES

God is our refuge and strength, a very present help in trouble.

Psalm 46:1 NKJV

Women of every generation have experienced adversity, and this generation is no different. But, today's women face challenges that previous generations could have scarcely imagined. Thankfully, although the world continues to change, God's love remains constant. And, He remains ready to comfort us and strengthen us whenever we turn to Him.

Psalm 147 promises, "He heals the brokenhearted, and binds their wounds" (v. 3). When we are troubled, we must call upon God, and, in His own time and according to His own plan, He will heal us.

If you're having tough times, don't hit the panic button and don't keep everything bottled up inside. Talk things over with people you can really trust.

If you are like most women, it is simply a fact of life: from time to time, you worry. You worry about health, about finances, about safety, about relationships, about family, and about countless other challenges of life, some great and some small. Where is the best place to take your worries? Take them to God. Take your troubles to Him, and your fears, and your sorrows. Seek protection from the One who cannot be moved.

FOOD FOR THOUGHT

If God sends us on stony paths, he provides strong shoes.

Corrie ten Boom

We all go through pain and sorrow, but the presence of God, like a warm, comforting blanket, can shield us and protect us, and allow the deep inner joy to surface, even in the most devastating circumstances.

Barbara Johnson

Add to your faith virtue; and to virtue, knowledge; and to knowledge, temperance; and to temperance, patience; and to patience, godliness; and to godliness, brotherly kindness; and to brotherly kindness, charity.

2 Peter 1:5-7 KJV

A HEALTHY-CHOICE TIP

If you're trying to remodel yourself, you'll need to remodel your environment, too. In order to decrease temptations and increase the probability of success, you should take a long, hard look at your home, your office, and the places you frequently visit. Then, you must do whatever you can to move yourself as far as possible from the temptations that you intend to defeat.

BIG DREAMS

With God's power working in us, God can do much, much more than anything we can ask or imagine.

Ephesians 3:20 NCV

Are you willing to entertain the possibility that God has big plans in store for you? Hopefully so. Yet sometimes, especially if you've recently experienced a life-altering disappointment, you may find it difficult to envision a brighter future for yourself and your family. If so, it's time to reconsider your own capabilities . . . and God's.

Your Heavenly Father created you with unique gifts and untapped talents; your job is to tap them. When you do, you'll begin to feel an increasing sense of confidence in yourself and in your future.

> You can dream big dreams, but you can never out-dream God. His plans for you are even bigger than you can imagine.

It takes courage to dream big dreams. You will discover that courage when you do three things: accept the past, trust God to handle the future, and make the most of the time He has given you today.

Nothing is too difficult for God, and no dreams are too big for Him—not even yours. So start living—and dreaming—accordingly.

FOOD FOR THOUGHT

Sometimes our dreams were so big that it took two people to dream them.

Marie T. Freeman

Always stay connected to people and seek out things that bring you joy. Dream with abandon. Pray confidently.

Barbara Johnson

The future lies all before us. Shall it only be a slight advance upon what we usually do? Ought it not to be a bound, a leap forward to altitudes of endeavor and success undreamed of before?

Annie Armstrong

Allow your dreams a place in your prayers and plans. God-given dreams can help you move into the future He is preparing for you.

Barbara Johnson

A HEALTHY-CHOICE TIP

Educate yourself on which foods are healthy and which foods aren't. Read labels and learn the basics of proper nutrition. Then, use common sense and discipline in planning your diet.

GOD'S PROTECTION

The Lord is my strength and my song; He has become my salvation.

Exodus 15:2 HCSB

In a world filled with dangers and temptations, God is the ultimate armor. In a world filled with misleading messages, God's Word is the ultimate truth. In a world filled with more frustrations than we can count, God's Son offers the ultimate peace. Will you accept God's peace and wear God's armor against the dangers of our world?

Sometimes, in the crush of everyday life, God may seem far away, but He is not. God is everywhere you have ever been and everywhere you will ever go. He is with you night and day; He knows your thoughts and your prayers. He is your ultimate Protector. And, when you earnestly seek His protection, you will find it because He is here—always—waiting patiently for you to reach out to Him.

Today, pray for God's protection and God's guidance. You need both.

FOOD FOR THOUGHT

God will never let you sink under your circumstances. He always provide a safety net and His love always encircles.

Barbara Johnson

Only believe, don't fear. Our Master, Jesus, always watches over us, and no matter what the persecution, Jesus will surely overcome it.

Lottie Moon

Our future may look fearfully intimidating, yet we can look up to the Engineer of the Universe, confident that nothing escapes His attention or slips out of the control of those strong hands.

Elisabeth Elliot

Worries carry responsibilities that belong to God, not to you. Worry does not enable us to escape evil; it makes us unfit to cope with it when it comes.

Corrie ten Boom

STRENGTHENING YOUR FAITH

You are protected by God . . . now and always. The only security that lasts is the security that flows from the loving heart of God.

YOUR BODY, YOUR CHOICES

So then each of us shall give account of himself to God.

Romans 14:12 NKJV

As adults, each of us bears a personal responsibility for the general state of our own physical health. Certainly, various aspects of health are beyond our control: illness sometimes strikes even the healthiest men and women. But for most of us, physical health is a choice: it is the result of hundreds of small decisions that we make every day of our lives. If we make decisions that promote good health, our bodies respond. But if we fall into bad habits and undisciplined lifestyles, we suffer tragic consequences.

God has entrusted you with the responsibility of caring for your body. So it's always the right time to become proactive about your health.

When our unhealthy habits lead to poor health, we find it all too easy to look beyond ourselves and assign blame. In fact, we live in a society where blame has become a national obsession: we blame cigarette manufacturers, restaurants, and food producers, to name only a few. But to blame others is to miss the point: we, and we alone, are responsible for the way that we treat our bodies. And the sooner that we accept that responsibility, the sooner we can assert control over our bodies and our lives.

Do you sincerely desire to improve your physical fitness? If so, start by taking personal responsibility for the body that God has given you. Then, make the solemn pledge to yourself that you will begin to make the changes that are required to enjoy a longer, healthier, happier life.

FOOD FOR THOUGHT

Even a child is known by his actions, by whether his conduct is pure and right.

Proverbs 20:11 NIV

Although God causes all things to work together for good for His children, He still holds us accountable for our behavior.

Kay Arthur

A HEALTHY-CHOICE TIP

It's easy to blame other people for the current state of your health. You live in a world where it's fashionable to blame food manufacturers, doctors, and fast food restaurants, to mention but a few. Yet none of these folks force food into your mouth, and they don't force you to sit on the sofa when you should be exercising! So remember: it's your body . . . and it's your responsibility.

HEALTHY PRIORITIES

Beloved, I pray that in all respects you may prosper and be in good health, just as your soul prospers.

3 John 1:2 NASB

When it comes to matters of physical, spiritual, and emotional health, Christians possess an infallible guidebook: the Holy Bible. And, when it comes to matters concerning fitness—whether physical, emotional, or spiritual fitness—God's Word can help us establish clear priorities that can guide our steps and our lives.

It's easy to talk about establishing clear priorities for maintaining physical and spiritual health, but it's much more difficult to live according to those priorities. For busy believers living in a demanding world, placing first things first can be difficult indeed. Why? Because so many people are expecting so many things from us!

Time is a non-renewable resource. Today, think about the ways to spend your time more wisely.

If you're having trouble prioritizing your day—or if you're having trouble sticking to a plan that enhances your spiritual and physical health—perhaps you've been trying to organize your life according to your own plans, not God's. A better strategy, of course, is to take your daily obligations and place them in the hands of the

One who created you. To do so, you must prioritize your day according to God's commandments, and you must seek His will and His wisdom in all matters.

FOOD FOR THOUGHT

Ultimate healing and the glorification of the body are certainly among the blessings of Calvary for the believing Christian. Immediate healing is not guaranteed.

Warren Wiersbe

A HEALTHY-CHOICE TIP

High blood pressure can cause heart attacks, strokes, and plenty of other serious health problems. The good news is that high blood pressure is usually treatable with medication, or lifestyle changes, or both. But you won't know you need treatment unless you know your blood pressure. Thankfully, blood pressure cuffs can be found just about everywhere, in many drug stores and even in some supermarkets. So remember this: you don't have to wait for a doctor's appointment to check your blood pressure. You can monitor your own blood pressure in between visits to the doctor's office, and that's precisely what you should do.

THE WORLD CHANGES, BUT GOD DOES NOT

There is a time for everything, and a season for every activity under heaven.

Ecclesiastes 3:1 NIV

Our world is in a state of constant change. God is not. At times, the world seems to be trembling beneath our feet. But we can be comforted in the knowledge that our Heavenly Father is the rock that cannot be shaken. His Word promises, "I am the Lord, I do not change" (Malachi 3:6 NKJV).

Change is inevitable; growth is not. God will come to your doorstep on countless occasions with opportunities to learn and to grow.

Every day that we live, we mortals encounter a multitude of changes—some good, some not so good. And on occasion, all of us must endure life-changing personal losses that leave us breathless. When we do, our loving Heavenly Father stands ready to protect us, to comfort us, to guide us, and, in time, to heal us.

Are you facing difficult circumstances or unwelcome changes? If so, please remember that God is far bigger than any problem you may face. So, instead of worrying about life's inevitable challenges, put your faith in the Father and His only begotten Son: "Jesus Christ is the same yesterday, today, and forever" (Hebrews 13:8 HCSB). And rest assured: It is precisely because your Savior does not change that you can face your challenges with courage for this day and hope for the future.

FOOD FOR THOUGHT

Mere change is not growth. Growth is the synthesis of change and continuity, and where there is no continuity there is no growth.

C. S. Lewis

With God, it isn't who you were that matters; it's who you are becoming.

Liz Curtis Higgs

More often than not, when something looks like it's the absolute end, it is really the beginning.

Charles Swindoll

STRENGTHENING YOUR FAITH

Your journey with God unfolds day by day, and that's precisely how your journey to an improved state of physical fitness must also unfold: moment by moment, day by day, year by year.

CHOOSING TO LET GOD TRANSFORM YOUR LIFE

Your old life is dead. Your new life, which is your real life—even though invisible to spectators—is with Christ in God. He is your life.

Colossians 3:3 MSG

Think, for a moment, about the "old" you, the person you were before you invited Christ to reign over your heart. Now, think about the "new" you, the person you have become since then. Is there a difference between the "old" you and the "new and improved" version? There should be! And that difference should be noticeable not only to you but also to others.

Unless you're a radically different person because of your relationship with Jesus, your faith isn't what it could be . . . or should be.

The Bible clearly teaches that when we welcome Christ into our hearts, we become new creations through Him. Our challenge, of course, is to behave ourselves like new creations. When we do, God fills our hearts, He blesses our endeavors, and transforms our lives . . . forever.

FOOD FOR THOUGHT

Repentance involves a radical change of heart and mind in which we agree with God's evaluation of our sin and then take specific action to align ourselves with His will.

Henry Blackaby

If we accept His invitation to salvation, we live with Him forever. However, if we do not accept because we refuse His only Son as our Savior, then we exclude ourselves from My Father's House. It's our choice.

Anne Graham Lotz

If you are God's child, you are no longer bound to your past or to what you were. You are a brand new creature in Christ Jesus.

Kay Arthur

There is so much Heaven around us now if we have eyes for it, because eternity starts when we give ourselves to God.

Gloria Gaither

A HEALTHY-CHOICE TIP

If you're serious about improving your fitness or your faith, pray about it.

GETTING ENOUGH REST?

Come to Me, all you who are weary and burdened, and I will give you rest.

Matthew 11:28-30 NKJV

Even the most inspired Christians can, from time to time, find themselves running on empty. The demands of daily life can drain us of our strength and rob us of the joy that is rightfully ours in Christ. When we find ourselves tired, discouraged, or worse, there is a source from which we can draw the power needed to recharge our spiritual batteries. That source is God.

God wants you to get enough rest. The world wants you to burn the candle at both ends. Trust God.

God intends that His children lead joyous lives filled with abundance and peace. But sometimes, abundance and peace seem very far away. It is then that we must turn to God for renewal, and when we do, He will restore us.

God expects us to work hard, but He also intends for us to rest. When we fail to take the rest that we need, we do a disservice to ourselves and to our families.

Is your spiritual battery running low? Is your energy on the wane? Are your emotions frayed? If so, it's time to turn your thoughts and your prayers to God. And when you're finished, it's time to rest.

FOOD FOR THOUGHT

And be not conformed to this world: but be ye transformed by the renewing of your mind.

Romans 12:2 KJV

And the apostles gathered themselves together unto Jesus, and told him all things, both what they had done, and what they had taught. And he said unto them, Come ye yourselves apart into a desert place, and rest a while.

Mark 6:30-31 HCSB

I will lift up mine eyes unto the hills, from whence cometh my help. My help cometh from the Lord, which made heaven and earth.

Psalm 121:1-2 KJV

A HEALTHY-CHOICE TIP

Most adults need about eight hours of sleep each night. If you're depriving yourself of much needed sleep in order to stay up and watch late night television, you've developed a bad habit. Instead, do yourself a favor: turn off the TV and go to bed.

DAY 34

THE TRAGEDY OF ADDICTION

Let us walk with decency, as in the daylight: not in carousing and drunkenness.

Romans 13:13 HCSB

The dictionary defines addiction as " the compulsive need for a habit-forming substance; the condition of being habitually and compulsively occupied with something." That definition is accurate, but incomplete. For Christians, addiction has an additional meaning: it means compulsively worshipping something other than God.

Ours is a highly addictive society. Why? The answer is straightforward: supply and demand. The supply of addictive substances continues to grow; the affordablity and availability of these substances makes them highly attractive to consumers; and the overall demand for addictive substances has increased as more users have become addicted to an ever-expanding array of substances and compulsions.

You must guard your heart against addiction . . . or else.

You know people who are full-blown addicts—probably lots of people. If you, or someone you love, is suffering from the blight of addiction, the following ideas are worth remembering:

1. For the addict, addiction comes first. In the life of an addict, addiction rules. God, of course, commands otherwise. God says, "You shall have no other gods before Me," and He means precisely what He says (Exodus 20:3 NKJV). Our task, as believers, is to put God in His proper place: first place. 2. You cannot cure another person's addiction, but you can encourage that person to seek help. Addicts are cured when they decide, not when you decide. What you can do is this: you can be supportive, and you can encourage the addict to find the help that he or she needs (Luke 10:25-37). 3. If you are living with an addicted person, think about safety: yours and your family's. Addiction is life-threatening and life-shortening. Don't let someone else's addiction threaten your safety or the safety of your loved ones (Proverbs 22:3). 4. Don't assist in prolonging the addiction: When you interfere with the negative consequences that might otherwise accompany an addict's negative behaviors, you are inadvertently "enabling" the addict to continue the destructive cycle of addiction. So don't be an enabler (Proverbs 15:31). 5. Help is available: Lots of people have experienced addiction and lived to tell about it. They want to help. Let them (Proverbs 27:17). 6. A cure is possible. With God's help, no addiction is incurable. And with God, no situation is hopeless (Matthew 19:26).

DAY 35

YOUR CHOICES MATTER

I am offering you life or death, blessings or curses. Now, choose life! . . . To choose life is to love the Lord your God, obey him, and stay close to him.

Deuteronomy 30:19-20 NCV

Each day, we make thousands of small choices concerning the things that we do and the things we think. Most of these choices are made without too much forethought. In fact, most of us go about our daily lives spending a significant portion of our lives simply reacting to events. Often, our actions are simply the result of impulse or habit. God asks that we slow down long enough to think about the choices that we make, and He asks that we make those choices in accordance with His commandments.

> First you make choices . . . and soon those choices begin to shape your life. That's why you must make smart choices . . . or face the consequences.

The Bible teaches us that our bodies are "temples" which belong to God (1 Corinthians 6:19-20). We are commanded (not encouraged, not advised, commanded!) to treat our bodies with respect and honor. We do so by making wise choices and by making those choices consistently over an extended period of time.

Do you sincerely seek to improve the overall quality of your health? Then vow to yourself and to God that you will begin making the kind of wise choices that will lead to a longer, healthier, happier life. The responsibility for those choices is yours. And so are the rewards.

FOOD FOR THOUGHT

Every day of our lives we make choices about how we're going to live that day.

Luci Swindoll

There may be no trumpet sound or loud applause when we make a right decision, just a calm sense of resolution and peace.

Gloria Gaither

A HEALTHY-CHOICE TIP

Do you think God wants you to develop healthy habits? Of course He does! Physical, emotional, and spiritual fitness are all part of God's plan for you. But it's up to you to make certain that a healthy lifestyle is a fundamental part of your plan, too.

THE POWER OF DAILY WORSHIP AND MEDITATION

Man shall not live by bread alone, but by every word that proceeds from the mouth of God.

Matthew 4:4 NKJV

Are you concerned about your spiritual, physical, or emotional fitness? If so, there is a timeless source of advice and comfort upon which you can—and should—depend. That source is the Holy Bible.

God's Word has much to say about every aspect of your life, including your health. If you face personal health challenges that seem almost insoluble, have faith and seek God's wisdom. If you can't seem to get yourself on a sensible diet or on a program of regular physical exercise, consult God's teachings. If your approach to your physical or emotional health has, up to this point, been undisciplined, pray for the strength to do what you know is right.

God's Word has the power to change every aspect of your life, including your health.

God has given you the Holy Bible for the purpose of knowing His promises, His power, His commandments, His wisdom, His love, and His Son. As you seek to improve the state of your own health, study God's teachings and apply them to your life. When you do, you will be blessed, now and forever.

FOOD FOR THOUGHT

He awakens Me morning by morning, He awakens My ear to hear as the learned. The Lord God has opened My ear.

Isaiah 50:4-5 NKJV

Lord, You are my lamp; the Lord illuminates my darkness.

2 Samuel 22:29 HCSB

Teach me Your way, Lord, and I will live by Your truth. Give me an undivided mind to fear Your name.

Psalm 86:11 HCSB

I will instruct you and show you the way to go; with My eye on you, I will give counsel.

Psalm 32:8 HCSB

STRENGTHENING YOUR FAITH

Find the best time of the day to spend with God. Hudson Taylor, an English missionary, wrote, "Whatever is your best time in the day, give that to communion with God." That's powerful advice that leads to a powerful faith.

FINDING CONTENTMENT

I am the door. If anyone enters by Me, he will be saved, and will come in and go out and find pasture.

John 10:9 HCSB

Where can you find contentment? Is it a result of wealth, or power, or beauty, or fame? Hardly. Genuine contentment springs from a peaceful spirit, a clear conscience, and a loving heart (like yours!).

Our modern world seems preoccupied with the search for happiness. We are bombarded with messages telling us that happiness depends upon the acquisition of material possessions. These messages are false. Enduring peace is not the result of our acquisitions; it is the inevitable result of our dispositions. If we don't find contentment within ourselves, we will never find it outside ourselves.

God offers you His peace, His protection, and His promises. If you accept these gifts, you will be content.

Thus the search for contentment is an internal quest, an exploration of the heart, mind, and soul. You can find contentment—indeed you will find it—if you simply look in the right places. And the best time to start looking in those places is now.

FOOD FOR THOUGHT

I believe that in every time and place it is within our power to acquiesce in the will of God—and what peace it brings to do so!

Elisabeth Elliot

The key to contentment is to consider. Consider who you are and be satisfied with that. Consider what you have and be satisfied with that. Consider what God's doing and be satisfied with that.

Luci Swindoll

Father and Mother lived on the edge of poverty, and yet their contentment was not dependent upon their surroundings. Their relationship to each other and to the Lord gave them strength and happiness.

Corrie ten Boom

STRENGTHENING YOUR FAITH

Be contented where you are, even if it's not exactly where you want to end up. God has something wonderful in store for you—and remember that God's timing is perfect—so be patient, trust God, do your best, and expect the best.

MAKING THE RIGHT CHOICES

A wise man will hear and increase learning, and a man of understanding will attain wise counsel.

Proverbs 1:5 NKJV

Life is a series of choices. Each day, we make countless decisions that can bring us closer to God . . . or not. When we live according to God's commandments, we earn for ourselves the abundance and peace that He intends for us to experience. But, when we turn our backs upon God by disobeying Him, we bring needless suffering upon ourselves and our families.

Today, think about unwise choices you've made in the past and wise choices you intend to make in the future.

Do you seek God's peace and His blessings? Then obey Him. When you're faced with a difficult choice or a powerful temptation, seek God's counsel and trust the counsel He gives. Invite God into your heart and live according to His commandments. When you do, you will be blessed today, tomorrow, and forever.

God has given you a guidebook for righteous living called the Holy Bible. It contains thorough instructions which, if followed, lead to fulfillment and salvation. But, if you choose to ignore God's commandments, the results are as predictable as they are tragic.

So here's a surefire formula for a happy, abundant life: live righteously.

And for further instructions, read the manual.

FOOD FOR THOUGHT

Wisdom is the God-given ability to see life with rare objectivity and to handle life with rare stability.

Charles Swindoll

Wisdom is knowledge applied. Head knowledge is useless on the battlefield. Knowledge stamped on the heart makes one wise.

Beth Moore

A HEALTHY-CHOICE TIP

John Maxwell observed, "The key to healthy eating is moderation and managing what you eat every day." And he was right. Crash diets don't usually work, but sensible eating habits do work, so plan your meals accordingly.

DAY 39

KNOW WHAT YOU EAT

Acquire wisdom—how much better it is than gold! And acquire understanding—it is preferable to silver.

Proverbs 16:16 HCSB

How hard is it for us to know the nutritional properties of the foods we eat? Not very hard. In the grocery store, almost every food item is clearly marked. In fast-food restaurants, the fat and calorie contents are posted on the wall (although the print is incredibly small, and with good reason: the health properties of these tasty tidbits are, in most cases, so poor that we should rename them "fat foods").

Today, make it a point to measure every calorie you consume. Then, at the end of the day, ask yourself if your food choices have been wise, unwise, or disastrous.

As informed adults, we have access to all the information that we need to make healthy dietary choices. Now it's up to each of us to make wise dietary choices, or not. Those choices are ours, and so are their consequences.

FOOD FOR THOUGHT

But also for this very reason, giving all diligence, add to your faith virtue, to virtue knowledge.

2 Peter 1:5 NKJV

Let the word of Christ dwell in you richly in all wisdom, teaching and admonishing one another in psalms and hymns and spiritual songs, singing with grace in your hearts to the Lord.

Colossians 3:16 NKJV

Those who are wise shall shine like the brightness of the firmament, and those who turn many to righteousness like the stars forever and ever.

Daniel 12:3 NKJV

STRENGTHENING YOUR FAITH

Wisdom 101: If you're looking for wisdom (health or otherwise), the Book of Proverbs is a wonderful place to start. It has 31 chapters, one for each day of the month. If you read Proverbs regularly, and if you take its teachings to heart, you'll gain timeless wisdom from God's unchanging Word.

THE FUTILITY OF BLAME

People's own foolishness ruins their lives, but in their minds they blame the Lord.

Proverbs 19:3 NCV

When our unhealthy habits lead to poor health, we find it all too easy to look beyond ourselves and assign blame. In fact, we live in a society where blame has become a national obsession: we blame cigarette manufacturers, restaurants, and food producers, to name only a few. But to blame others is to miss the point: we, and we alone, are responsible for the way that we treat our bodies. And the sooner that we accept that responsibility, the sooner we can assert control over our bodies and our lives.

Today, ask God to help you take responsibility for the current state of your health. And while you're at it, ask Him to help you make wise choices in the future.

So, when it comes to your own body, assume control and accept responsibility. It's a great way to live and a great way to stay healthy.

FOOD FOR THOUGHT

The main thing is this: we should never blame anyone or anything for our defeats. No matter how evil their intentions may be, they are altogether unable to harm us until we begin to blame them and use them as excuses for our own unbelief.

A. W. Tozer

The single most important element in any human relationship is honesty—with oneself, with God, and with others.

Catherine Marshall

Never use your problem as an excuse for bad attitudes or behavior.

Joyce Meyer

A HEALTHY-CHOICE TIP

The road to poor health is paved with good intentions. Until you make exercise a high priority in your life, your good intentions will soon give way to old habits. So give your exercise regimen a position of high standing on your daily to-do list.

SENSIBLE EXERCISE

No discipline seems pleasant at the time, but painful. Later on, however, it produces a harvest of righteousness and peace for those who have been trained by it.

Hebrews 12:11 NIV

A healthy lifestyle includes regular, sensible physical exercise. How much exercise is right for you? That's a decision that you should make in consultation with your physician. But make no mistake: if you sincerely desire to be a thoughtful caretaker of the body that God has given you, exercise is important.

God rewards wise behaviors and He punishes misbehavior. A commitment to a sensible exercise program is one way of being wise, and it's also one way of pleasing God.

Once you begin a regular exercise program, you'll discover that the benefits to you are not only physical but also psychological. Regular exercise allows you to build your muscles while you're clearing your head and lifting your spirits.

So, if you've been taking your body for granted, today is a wonderful day to change. You can start slowly, perhaps with a brisk walk around the block. As your stamina begins to build, so will your sense of satisfaction. And, you'll be comforted by the knowledge that you've done your part to protect and preserve the precious body that God has entrusted to your care.

FOOD FOR THOUGHT

The effective Christians of history have been men and women of great personal discipline—mental discipline, discipline of the body, discipline of the tongue, and discipline of the emotion.

Billy Graham

Sow righteousness for yourselves and reap faithful love; break up your untilled ground. It is time to seek the Lord until He comes and sends righteousness on you like the rain.

Hosea 10:12 HCSB

Don't you know that you are God's temple and that God's Spirit lives in you?

1 Corinthians 3:16 NCV

A HEALTHY-CHOICE TIP

Make exercise enjoyable. Your workouts should be a source of pleasure and satisfaction, not a form of self-imposed punishment. Find a way to exercise your body that is satisfying, effective, and fun.

DAY 42

SPIRITUAL HEALTH, SPIRITUAL GROWTH

But the fruit of the Spirit is love, joy, peace, long-suffering, gentleness, goodness, faith, meekness, temperance . . . .

Galatians 5:22-23 KJV

Are you as "spiritually fit" as you're ever going to be? Hopefully not! When it comes to your faith (and, by the way, when it comes to your fitness), God isn't done with you yet.

The journey toward spiritual maturity lasts a lifetime: As Christians, we can and should continue to grow in the love and the knowledge of our Savior as long as we live. But, if we cease to grow, either emotionally or spiritually, we do ourselves and our families a profound disservice.

> Wherever you are in your spiritual journey, it's always the right time to take another step toward God.

If we study God's Word, if we obey His commandments, and if we live in the center of His will, we will not be "stagnant" believers; we will, instead, be growing Christians . . . and that's exactly what God wants for our lives.

In those quiet moments when we open our hearts to God, the Creator who made us keeps remaking us. He gives us direction, perspective, wisdom, and courage. He encourages us to become more fit in a variety of ways: more spiritually fit, more physically fit, and more emotionally fit.

God is willing to do His part to ensure that you remain fit. Are you willing to do yours?

FOOD FOR THOUGHT

If all struggles and sufferings were eliminated, the spirit would no more reach maturity than would the child.

Elisabeth Elliot

We set our eyes on the finish line, forgetting the past, and straining toward the mark of spiritual maturity and fruitfulness.

Vonette Bright

STRENGTHENING YOUR FAITH

Spiritual growth is not instantaneous . . . and neither, for that matter, is the attainment of a physically fit body. So be patient. You should expect a few ups and downs along the way, but you should also expect to see progress over time.

HAVE THE COURAGE TO TRUST GOD

Trust in the Lord with all your heart, and do not rely on your own understanding; think about Him in all your ways, and He will guide you on the right paths.

Proverbs 3:5-6 HCSB

When our dreams come true and our plans prove successful, we find it easy to thank our Creator and easy to trust His divine providence. But in times of sorrow or hardship, we may find ourselves questioning God's plans for our lives.

On occasion, you will confront circumstances that trouble you to the very core of your soul. It is during these difficult days that you must find the wisdom and the courage to trust your Heavenly Father despite your circumstances.

Are you a woman who seeks God's blessings for yourself and your family? Then trust Him. Trust Him with your relationships. Trust Him with your priorities. Follow His commandments and pray for His guidance. Trust Your Heavenly Father day by day, moment by moment—in good times and in trying times.

> What is courage? It is the ability to be strong in trust, in conviction, in obedience. To be courageous is to step out in faith— to trust and obey, no matter what.
>
> *Kay Arthur*

Then, wait patiently for God's revelations . . . and prepare yourself for the abundance and peace that will most certainly be yours when you do.

FOOD FOR THOUGHT

Sometimes the very essence of faith is trusting God in the midst of things He knows good and well we cannot comprehend.

Beth Moore

Are you serious about wanting God's guidance to become the person he wants you to be? The first step is to tell God that you know you can't manage your own life; that you need his help.

Catherine Marshall

Brother, is your faith looking upward today? / Trust in the promise of the Savior. / Sister, is the light shining bright on your way? / Trust in the promise of thy Lord.

Fanny Crosby

STRENGTHENING YOUR FAITH

Because God is trustworthy—and because He has made promises to you that He intends to keep—you are protected.

IN SEARCH OF WISDOM AND BALANCE

Now if any of you lacks wisdom, he should ask God, who gives to all generously and without criticizing, and it will be given to him. But let him ask in faith without doubting. For the doubter is like the surging sea, driven and tossed by the wind.

James 1:5-6 HCSB

To find balance, you must find wisdom. Where will you find wisdom today? Will you seek it from God or from the world? As a thoughtful woman living in a society that is filled with temptations and distractions, you know that the world's brand of "wisdom" is everywhere . . . and it is dangerous. You live in a world where it's all too easy to stray far from the ultimate source of wisdom: God's Holy Word.

God makes His wisdom available to you. Your job is to acknowledge, to understand, and (above all) to use that wisdom.

When you commit yourself to the daily study of God's Word—and when you live according to His commandments—you will become wise . . . in time. But don't expect to open your Bible today and be wise tomorrow. Wisdom is not like a mushroom; it does not spring up overnight. It is, instead, like a majestic oak tree that starts as a tiny acorn, grows into a sapling, and eventually reaches up to the sky, tall and strong.

Today and every day, as a way of understanding God's plan for your life, you should study His Word and live by it. When you do, you will accumulate a storehouse of wisdom that will enrich your own life and the lives of your family members, your friends, and the world.

FOOD FOR THOUGHT

This is my song through endless ages: Jesus led me all the way.

Fanny Crosby

If we neglect the Bible, we cannot expect to benefit from the wisdom and direction that result from knowing God's Word.

Vonette Bright

Knowledge can be found in books or in school. Wisdom, on the other hand, starts with God . . . and ends there.

Marie T. Freeman

A HEALTHY-CHOICE TIP

An exercise program that starts slowly and builds over time is far better than an exercise program that starts—and ends—quickly.

PRAY CONSTANTLY

Rejoice in hope; be patient in affliction; be persistent in prayer.
Romans 12:12 HCSB

God's Word promises that prayer is a powerful tool for changing your life and your world. So here's a question: Are you using prayer as a powerful tool to improve your world, or are you praying sporadically at best? If you're wise, you've learned that prayer is indeed powerful and that it is most powerful when it is used often.

Prayer changes things—and you—so pray.

Today, if you haven't already done so, establish the habit of praying constantly. Don't pray day-to-day; pray hour-to-hour. Start each day with prayer, end it with prayer, and fill it with prayer. That's the best way to know God; it's the best way to change your world; and it is, quite simply, the best way to live.

FOOD FOR THOUGHT

What God gives in answer to our prayers will always be the thing we most urgently need, and it will always be sufficient.

Elisabeth Elliot

Your family and friends need your prayers and you need theirs. And God wants to hear those prayers. So what are you waiting for?

Marie T. Freeman

We must leave it to God to answer our prayers in His own wisest way. Sometimes, we are so impatient and think that God does not answer. God always answers! He never fails! Be still. Abide in Him.

Mrs. Charles E. Cowman

Is anyone among you suffering? He should pray. Is anyone cheerful? He should sing praises.

James 5:13 HCSB

STRENGTHENING YOUR FAITH

Don't ever be embarrassed to pray: Are you embarrassed to bow your head in a restaurant? Don't be; it's the people who aren't praying who should be embarrassed!

DAY 46

PROTECTING YOUR EMOTIONAL HEALTH

And the peace of God, which surpasses every thought, will guard your hearts and your minds in Christ Jesus. Finally brothers, whatever is true, whatever is honorable, whatever is just, whatever is pure, whatever is lovely, whatever is commendable—if there is any moral excellence and if there is any praise—dwell on these things.

Philippians 4:7-8 HCSB

Emotional health isn't simply the absence of sadness; it's also the ability to enjoy life and the wisdom to celebrate God's gifts. Christians have every reason to be optimistic about life. As John Calvin observed, "There is not one blade of grass, there is no color in this world that is not intended to make us rejoice." But sometimes, when we are tired or frustrated, rejoicing seems only a distant promise. Thankfully, God stands ready to restore us: "I will give you a new heart and put a new spirit in you...." (Ezekiel 36:26 NIV). Our task, of course, is to let Him.

> When negative emotions threaten to hijack your day, lift your thoughts—and your prayers—to God.

If you're feeling deeply discouraged or profoundly depressed, then it is time to seriously address the state of your emotional health. First, open your heart to God in prayer. Then, talk with trusted family members, friends, and your pastor. And, if you or someone close to you considers it wise, seek advice from your physician or make an appointment with a licensed mental health professional.

When your emotional health is at stake, you should avail yourself of every reasonable resource. Then, armed with the promises of your Creator and the support of family and friends, you can go about the business of solving the challenges that confront you. When you do, the clouds will eventually part, and the sun will shine once more upon your soul.

FOOD FOR THOUGHT

Worry does not empty tomorrow of its sorrow; it empties today of its strength.

Corrie ten Boom

A HEALTHY-CHOICE TIP

John Maxwell observed, "The key to healthy eating is moderation and managing what you eat every day." And he was right. Crash diets don't usually work, but sensible eating habits do work, so plan your meals accordingly.

TRUSTING GOD'S WILL

God is my shield, saving those whose hearts are true and right.
Psalm 7:10 NLT

God has will, and so do we. He gave us the power to make choices for ourselves, and He created a world in which those choices have consequences. The ultimate choice that we face, of course, is what to do about God. We can cast our lot with Him by choosing Jesus Christ as our personal Savior, or not. The choice is ours alone.

We also face thousands of small choices that make up the fabric of daily life. When we align those choices with God's commandments, and when we align our lives with God's will, we receive His abundance, His peace, and His joy. But when we struggle against God's will for our lives, we reap a bitter harvest indeed.

> When God's will becomes your will, good things happen.

Today, you'll face thousands of small choices; as you do, use God's Word as your guide. And, as you face the ultimate choice, place God's Son and God's will and God's love at the center of your life. You'll discover that God's plan is far grander than any you could have imagined.

FOOD FOR THOUGHT

To yield to God means to belong to God, and to belong to God means to have all His infinite power. To belong to God means to have all.

Hannah Whitall Smith

The will of God is never exactly what you expect it to be. It may seem to be much worse, but in the end it's going to be a lot better and a lot bigger.

Elisabeth Elliot

The center of power is not to be found in summit meetings or in peace conferences. It is not in Peking or Washington or the United Nations, but rather where a child of God prays in the power of the Spirit for God's will to be done in her life, in her home, and in the world around her.

Ruth Bell Graham

A HEALTHY-CHOICE TIP

Exercising discipline should never be viewed as an imposition or as a form of punishment; far from it. Discipline is the means by which you can take control of your life (which, by the way, is far better than letting your life control you).

FOLLOW HIM

If anyone serves Me, let him follow Me; and where I am, there My servant will be also. If anyone serves Me, him My Father will honor.

John 12:26 NKJV

Jesus walks with you. Are you walking with Him? Hopefully, you will choose to walk with Him today and every day of your life.

Jesus loved you so much that He endured unspeakable humiliation and suffering for you. How will you respond to Christ's sacrifice? Will you take up His cross and follow Him (Luke 9:23), or will you choose another path? When you place your hopes squarely at the foot of the cross, when you place Jesus squarely at the center of your life, you will be blessed. If you seek to be a worthy disciple of Jesus, you must acknowledge that He never comes "next." He is always first.

> It takes a genuine commitment—and significant sacrifices—to really follow Jesus. And it's worth it.

Do you hope to fulfill God's purpose for your life? Do you seek a life of abundance and peace? Do you intend to be Christian, not just in name, but in deed? Then follow Christ. Follow Him by picking up His cross today and every day that you live. When you do, you will quickly discover that Christ's love has the power to change everything, including you.

FOOD FOR THOUGHT

Will you, with a glad and eager surrender, hand yourself and all that concerns you over into his hands? If you will do this, your soul will begin to know something of the joy of union with Christ.

Hannah Whitall Smith

Peter said, "No, Lord!" But he had to learn that one cannot say "No" while saying "Lord" and that one cannot say "Lord" while saying "No."

Corrie ten Boom

The love life of the Christian is a crucial battleground. There, if nowhere else, it will be determined who is Lord: the world, the self, and the devil—or the Lord Christ.

Elisabeth Elliot

STRENGTHENING YOUR FAITH

Following Christ is a matter of obedience. If you want to be a little more like Jesus . . . learn about His teachings, follow in His footsteps, and obey His commandments.

START MAKING CHANGES NOW

But be doers of the word and not hearers only.

James 1:22 HCSB

Warren Wiersbe correctly observed, "A Christian should no more defile his body than a Jew would defile the temple." Unfortunately, too many of us have allowed our temples to fall into disrepair. When it comes to fitness and food, it's easy to fall into bad habits. And it's easy to convince ourselves that we'll start improving our health "some day."

Today, pick out one important obligation that you've been putting off. Then, take at least one specific step toward the completion of the task you've been avoiding.

If we are to care for our bodies in the way that God intends, we must establish healthy habits, and we must establish them sooner rather than later.

Saint Jerome advised, "Begin to be now what you will be hereafter." You should take his advice seriously, and you should take it NOW. When it comes to your health, it's always the right time to start establishing the right habits.

FOOD FOR THOUGHT

Let us not be content to wait and see what will happen, but give us the determination to make the right things happen.

Peter Marshall

Therefore, get your minds ready for action, being self-disciplined, and set your hope completely on the grace to be brought to you at the revelation of Jesus Christ.

1 Peter 1:13 HCSB

When you make a vow to God, don't delay fulfilling it, because He does not delight in fools. Fulfill what you vow.

Ecclesiastes 5:4 HCSB

For the hearers of the law are not righteous before God, but the doers of the law will be declared righteous.

Romans 2:13 HCSB

A HEALTHY-CHOICE TIP

When important work needs to be done, it's tempting to procrastinate. But God's Word teaches us to be "doers of the Word," which means taking action even when we might prefer to do nothing.

DAY 50

BE ENTHUSIASTIC

Whatever you do, do it enthusiastically, as something done for the Lord and not for men.

Colossians 3:23 HCSB

Are you passionate about your faith, your fitness, and your future? Hopefully so. But if your zest for life has waned, it is now time to redirect your efforts and recharge your spiritual batteries. And that means refocusing your priorities by putting God first.

Look at your life and your challenges as exciting adventures. Don't wait for life to spice itself; spice things up yourself.

Each day is a glorious opportunity to serve God and to do His will. Are you enthused about life, or do you struggle through each day giving scarcely a thought to God's blessings? Are you constantly praising God for His gifts, and are you sharing His Good News with the world? And are you excited about the possibilities for service that God has placed before you, whether at home, at work, or at church? You should be.

Nothing is more important than your wholehearted commitment to your Creator and to His only begotten Son. Your faith must never be an afterthought; it must be your ultimate priority, your ultimate possession, and your ultimate passion. When you become passionate about your faith, you'll become passionate about your life, too.

FOOD FOR THOUGHT

God is the giver, and we are the receivers. And His richest gifts are bestowed not upon those who do the greatest things, but upon those who accept His abundance and His grace.

Hannah Whitall Smith

Living life with a consistent spiritual walk deeply influences those we love most.

Vonette Bright

A HEALTHY-CHOICE TIP

You don't have to attend medical school to understand the basic principles of maintaining a healthy lifestyle. In fact, many of the things you need to know are contained in this text. But don't stop here. Vow to make yourself an expert on the care and feeding of the body that God has given you. In today's information-packed world, becoming an expert isn't a very hard thing to do.

DON'T OVERESTIMATE THE IMPORTANCE OF APPEARANCES

Man does not see what the Lord sees, for man sees what is visible, but the Lord sees the heart.

1 Samuel 16:7 HCSB

Are you worried about keeping up appearances? And as a result, do you spend too much time, energy, or money on things that are intended to make you look good? If so, you are certainly not alone. Ours is a society that focuses intently upon appearances. We are told time and again that we can't be "too thin or too rich." But in truth, the important things in life have little to do with food, fashion, fame, or fortune.

> How you appear to other people doesn't make much difference, but how you appear to God makes all the difference.

Today, spend less time trying to please the world and more time trying to please your earthly family and your Father in heaven. Focus today on pleasing your God and your loved ones, and don't worry too much about trying to impress the folks you happen to pass on the street. It takes too much energy—and too much life—to keep up appearances. So don't waste your energy or your life.

FOOD FOR THOUGHT

Comparison is the root of all feelings of inferiority.

James Dobson

Fashion is an enduring testimony to the fact that we live quite consciously before the eyes of others.

John Eldredge

Outside appearances, things like the clothes you wear or the car you drive, are important to other people but totally unimportant to God. Trust God.

Marie T. Freeman

If the narrative of the Scriptures teaches us anything, from the serpent in the Garden to the carpenter in Nazareth, it teaches us that things are rarely what they seem, that we shouldn't be fooled by appearances.

John Eldredge

STRENGTHENING YOUR FAITH

If you find yourself focussing too much on your appearance, it's time to find a different focus.

THE DECISION TO CELEBRATE LIFE

This is the day the Lord has made; let us rejoice and be glad in it.

Psalm 118:24 HCSB

God gives us this day; He fills it to the brim with possibilities, and He challenges us to use it for His purposes. The 118th Psalm reminds us that today, like every other day, is a cause for celebration. The day is presented to us fresh and clean at midnight, free of charge, but we must beware: Today is a non-renewable resource—once it's gone, it's gone forever. Our responsibility, of course, is to use this day in the service of God's will and according to His commandments.

By celebrating the gift of life, you protect your heart from the dangers of pessimism, regret, hopelessness, and bitterness.

Today, treasure the time that God has given you. Give Him the glory and the praise and the thanksgiving that He deserves. And search for the hidden possibilities that God has placed along your path. This day is a priceless gift from God, so use it joyfully and encourage others to do likewise. After all, this is the day the Lord has made.

FOOD FOR THOUGHT

Christ is the secret, the source, the substance, the center, and the circumference of all true and lasting gladness.

Mrs. Charles E. Cowman

When the dream of our heart is one that God has planted there, a strange happiness flows into us. At that moment, all of the spiritual resources of the universe are released to help us. Our praying is then at one with the will of God and becomes a channel for the Creator's purposes for us and our world.

Catherine Marshall

If you can forgive the person you were, accept the person you are, and believe in the person you will become, you are headed for joy. So celebrate your life.

Barbara Johnson

STRENGTHENING YOUR FAITH

God has given you the gift of life (here on earth) and the promise of eternal life (in heaven). Now, He wants you to celebrate those gifts.

BE A CHEERFUL CHRISTIAN

A cheerful heart has a continual feast.

Proverbs 15:15 HCSB

On some days, as every woman knows, it's hard to be cheerful. Sometimes, as the demands of the world increase and our energy sags, we feel less like "cheering up" and more like "tearing up." But even in our darkest hours, we can turn to God, and He will give us comfort.

Few things in life are more sad, or, for that matter, more absurd, than a grumpy Christian. Christ promises us lives of abundance and joy, but He does not force His joy upon us. We must claim His joy for ourselves, and when we do, Jesus, in turn, fills our spirits with His power and His love.

> Cheerfulness is its own reward—but not its only reward.

How can we receive from Christ the joy that is rightfully ours? By giving Him what is rightfully His: our hearts and our souls.

When we earnestly commit ourselves to the Savior of mankind, and when we place Jesus at the center of our lives and trust Him as our personal Savior, He will transform us, not just for today, but for all eternity. Then we, as God's children, can share Christ's joy and His message with a world that needs both.

FOOD FOR THOUGHT

Joy is the serious business of heaven.

C. S. Lewis

God is good, and heaven is forever. And if those two facts don't cheer you up, nothing will.

Marie T. Freeman

We may run, walk, stumble, drive, or fly, but let us never lose sight of the reason for the journey, or miss a chance to see a rainbow on the way.

Gloria Gaither

When we bring sunshine into the lives of others, we're warmed by it ourselves. When we spill a little happiness, it splashes on us.

Barbara Johnson

A HEALTHY-CHOICE TIP

God has given you many blessings, and you have many reasons to be cheerful. So what are you waiting for?

ASK HIM FOR THE THINGS YOU NEED

You do not have because you do not ask.

James 4:2 HCSB

God gives the gifts; we, as believers, should accept them—but oftentimes, we don't. Why? Because we fail to trust our Heavenly Father completely, and because we are, at times, surprisingly stubborn. Luke 11 teaches us that God does not withhold spiritual gifts from those who ask. Our obligation, quite simply, is to ask for them.

If you sincerely want to find balance, ask for God's help.

Are you a woman who asks God to move mountains in your life, or are you expecting Him to stumble over molehills? Whatever the size of your challenges, God is big enough to handle them. Ask for His help today, with faith and with fervor, and then watch in amazement as your mountains begin to move.

FOOD FOR THOUGHT

Often I have made a request of God with earnest pleadings even backed up with Scripture, only to have Him say "No" because He had something better in store.

Ruth Bell Graham

By asking in Jesus' name, we're making a request not only in His authority, but also for His interests and His benefit.

Shirley Dobson

When will we realize that we're not troubling God with our questions and concerns? His heart is open to hear us—his touch nearer than our next thought—as if no one in the world existed but us. Our very personal God wants to hear from us personally.

Gigi Graham Tchividjian

A HEALTHY-CHOICE TIP

If you want more from life, ask more from God. If you're searching for peace and abundance, ask for God's help—and keep asking—until He answers your prayers. If you sincerely want to rise above the stresses and complications of everyday life, ask for God's help many times each day.

GOD'S PLAN FOR YOUR HEALTH

Who are those who fear the Lord? He will show them the path they should choose. They will live in prosperity, and their children will inherit the Promised Land.

Psalm 25:12-13 NLT

The journey toward improved health is not only a common-sense exercise in personal discipline, it is also a spiritual journey ordained by our Creator. God does not intend that we abuse our bodies by giving in to excessive appetites or to slothful behavior. To the contrary, God has instructed us to protect our physical bodies to the greatest extent we can. To do otherwise is to disobey Him.

God has a plan for your spiritual, physical, and emotional health.

When you make the decision to seek God's will for your life—and you should—then you will contemplate His Word, and you will be watchful for His signs. God intends to use you in wonderful, unexpected ways if you let Him. But be forewarned: the decision to seek God's plan and fulfill His purpose is ultimately a decision that you must make by yourself and for yourself. The consequences of that decision have implications that are both profound and eternal, so choose carefully. And then, as you go about your daily activities, keep your eyes and ears open, as well as your heart, because God is patiently trying to get His message through . . . and there's no better moment than this one for you to help Him.

FOOD FOR THOUGHT

God has a plan for the life of every Christian. Every circumstance, every turn of destiny, all things work together for your good and for His glory.

Billy Graham

God's all-sufficiency is a major. Your inability is a minor. Major in majors, not in minors.

Corrie ten Boom

A HEALTHY-CHOICE TIP

We live in a junk-food society, but you shouldn't let your house become junk-food heaven. Make your home a haven of healthy foods. And remember, it's never too soon to teach your kid good habits . . . and that includes the very good habit of sensible eating.

YOU'RE ACCOUNTABLE

But each person should examine his own work, and then he will have a reason for boasting in himself alone, and not in respect to someone else. For each person will have to carry his own load.

Galatians 6:4-5 HCSB

We humans are masters at passing the buck. Why? Because passing the buck is easier than fixing, and criticizing others is so much easier than improving ourselves. So instead of solving our problems legitimately (by doing the work required to solve them) we are inclined to fret, to blame, and to criticize, while doing precious little else. When we do, our problems, quite predictably, remain unsolved.

It's easy to hold other people accountable, but real accountability begins with the person in the mirror.

Whether you like it or not, you (and only you) are accountable for your actions. But because you are human, you'll be sorely tempted to pass the blame. Avoid that temptation at all costs.

Problem-solving builds character. Every time you straighten your back and look squarely into the face of Old Man Trouble, you'll strengthen not only your backbone but also your spirit. So, instead of looking for someone to blame, look for something to fix, and then get busy fixing it. And as you consider your own situation, remember this: God has a way of helping those who help themselves, but He doesn't spend much time helping those who don't.

FOOD FOR THOUGHT

Generally speaking, accountability is a willingness to share our activities, conduct, and fulfillment of assigned responsibilities with others.

Charles Stanley

We urgently need people who encourage and inspire us to move toward God and away from the world's enticing pleasures.

Jim Cymbala

STRENGTHENING YOUR FAITH

If you want to build character, you need to assume responsibility for your actions. Once you begin to hold yourself accountable, you'll begin to grow emotionally and spiritually.

PUT FAITH ABOVE FEELINGS

Now the just shall live by faith.

Hebrews 10:38 NKJV

Who is in charge of your emotions? Is it you, or have you formed the unfortunate habit of letting other people— or troubling situations—determine the quality of your thoughts and the direction of your day? If you're wise— and if you'd like to build a better life for yourself and your loved ones—you'll learn to control your emotions before your emotions control you.

Here are the facts: God's love is real; His peace is real; His support is real. Don't ever let your emotions obscure these facts.

Human emotions are highly variable, decidedly unpredictable, and often unreliable. Our emotions are like the weather, only far more fickle. So we must learn to live by faith, not by the ups and downs of our own emotional roller coasters.

Sometime during this day, you will probably be gripped by a strong negative feeling. Distrust it. Reign it in. Test it. And turn it over to God. Your emotions will inevitably change; God will not. So trust Him completely as you watch those negative feelings slowly evaporate into thin air—which, of course, they will.

FOOD FOR THOUGHT

The only serious mistake we can make is the mistake that Psalm 121 prevents: the mistake of supposing that God's interest in us waxes and wanes in response to our spiritual temperature.

Eugene Peterson

Before you can dry another's tears, you too must weep.

Barbara Johnson

I may no longer depend on pleasant impulses to bring me before the Lord. I must rather respond to principles I know to be right, whether I feel them to be enjoyable or not.

Jim Elliot

Emotions we have not poured out in the safe hands of God can turn into feelings of hopelessness and depression. God is safe.

Beth Moore

A HEALTHY-CHOICE TIP

Fitness is a journey, not a destination. Achieving physical fitness—and maintaining it—is a seven-day-a-week assignment. If you don't make physical fitness a priority, your health will suffer.

MAKE THE MOST OF WHATEVER COMES

A man's heart plans his way, but the Lord determines his steps.
Proverbs 16:9 HCSB

Sometimes, we must accept life on its terms, not our own. Life has a way of unfolding, not as we will, but as it will. And sometimes, there is precious little we can do to change things.

When events transpire that are beyond our control, we have a choice: we can either learn the art of acceptance, or we can make ourselves miserable as we struggle to change the unchangeable.

> When you encounter situations that you cannot change, you must learn the wisdom of acceptance . . . and you must learn to trust God.

We must entrust the things we cannot change to God. Once we have done so, we can prayerfully and faithfully tackle the important work that He has placed before us: doing something about the things we can change . . . and doing it sooner rather than later.

Can you summon the courage and the wisdom to accept life on its own terms? If so, you'll most certainly be rewarded for your good judgment.

FOOD FOR THOUGHT

We must meet our disappointments, our persecutions, our malicious enemies, our provoking friends, our trials and temptations of every sort, with an attitude of surrender and trust. We must spread our wings and "mount up" to the "heavenly places in Christ" above them all, where they will lose their power to harm or distress us.

Hannah Whitall Smith

The one true way of dying to self is the way of patience, meekness, humility, and resignation to God.

Andrew Murray

It is always possible to do the will of God. In every place and time it is within our power to acquiesce in the will of God.

Elisabeth Elliot

A HEALTHY-CHOICE TIP

If you're genuinely planning on becoming a disciplined person "some day" in the distant future, you're deluding yourself. The best day to begin exercising self-discipline is this one.

RECHARGING YOUR SPIRITUAL BATTERIES

Those who hope in the LORD will renew their strength. They will soar on wings like eagles; they will run and not grow weary, they will walk and not be faint

Isaiah 40:31 NIV

As you make the journey toward improved fitness, you'll undoubtedly run out of energy from time to time. When it happens, you can turn to God for strength and for guidance.

For the journey through life, you need energy. If you're wise, you'll ask the Creator to energize you and guide you.

Andrew Murray observed, "Where there is much prayer, there will be much of the Spirit; where there is much of the Spirit, there will be ever-increasing power." These words remind us that the ultimate source of our strength is God. When we turn to Him—for guidance, for enlightenment, and for strength—we will not be disappointed.

Are you feeling exhausted? Are your emotions on edge? If so, it's time to turn things over to God in prayer. Are you weak or worried? Take the time—or, more accurately, make the time—to delve deeply into God's Holy Word. Are you spiritually depleted? Call upon fellow believers to support you, and call upon Christ to renew your spirit and your life. When you do, you'll discover that the Creator of the universe has the power to make all things new . . . including you.

FOOD FOR THOUGHT

Jesus taught us by example to get out of the rat race and recharge our batteries.

Barbara Johnson

Troubles we bear trustfully can bring us a fresh vision of God and a new outlook on life, an outlook of peace and hope.

Billy Graham

A HEALTHY-CHOICE TIP

God wants you to experience abundant life, but He will not force you to adopt a healthy lifestyle. Managing your food and your fitness is up to you.

If you want more from life, ask more from God. D. L. Moody observed, "Some people think God does not like to be troubled with our constant asking. But, the way to trouble God is not to come at all." So, if you seek an improved level of fitness—or if you seek any other worthy goal—ask God (and keep asking Him) until He answers your prayers.

DAY 60

PERSPECTIVE AND BALANCE

Come to Me, all you who labor and are heavy laden, and I will give you rest. Take My yoke upon you and learn from Me, for I am gentle and lowly in heart, and you will find rest for your souls. For My yoke is easy and My burden is light.

Matthew 11:28-30 NKJV

Sometimes, amid the demands of daily life, we lose perspective. Life seems out of balance, and the pressures of everyday living seem overwhelming. What's needed is a fresh perspective, a restored sense of balance...and God.

> Life is a balancing act. To improve your balance, consult your Heavenly Father many times each day.

If a temporary loss of perspective has robbed you of the spiritual fitness that should be yours in Christ, it's time to re-adjust your thought patterns. Negative thoughts are habit-forming; thankfully, so are positive ones. With practice, you can form the habit of focusing on God's priorities and your possibilities. When you do, you'll soon discover that you will spend less time fretting about your challenges and more time praising God for His gifts.

When you call upon the Lord and prayerfully seek His will, He will give you wisdom and perspective. When you make God's priorities your priorities, He will direct your steps and calm your fears. So today and every day hereafter, pray for a sense of balance and perspective. And remember: your thoughts are intensely powerful things, so handle them with care.

FOOD FOR THOUGHT

Prescription for a happier and healthier life: resolve to slow down your pace; learn to say no gracefully; resist the temptation to chase after more pleasure, more hobbies, and more social entanglements.

James Dobson

Notice what Jesus had to say concerning those who have wearied themselves by trying to do things in their own strength: "Come to me, all you who labor and are heavy laden, and I will give you rest."

Henry Blackaby and Claude King

A HEALTHY-CHOICE TIP

Need balance? Have a daily planning session with God. A regularly scheduled time of prayer, Bible reading, and meditation can help you prioritize your day and your life. And what if you're simply too busy to spend five or ten minutes with God? If so, it's time to reorder your priorities.

BEYOND THE SETBACKS

Peace, peace to you, and peace to him who helps you, for your God helps you.

1 Chronicles 12:18 HCSB

It's simply a fact of life: Not all of your health-related plans will succeed, and not all of your goals will be met. Life's occasional setbacks are simply the price that we must pay for our willingness to take risks as we follow our dreams. But even when we encounter bitter disappointments, we must never lose faith.

Remember that failure isn't permanent . . . unless you fail to get up. So pick yourself up, dust yourself off, and trust God.

Hebrews 10:36 advises, "Patient endurance is what you need now, so you will continue to do God's will. Then you will receive all that he has promised" (NLT). These words remind us that when we persevere, we will eventually receive the rewards which God has promised us. What's required is perseverance, not perfection.

When we face hardships, God stands ready to protect us. Our responsibility, of course, is to ask Him for protection. When we call upon Him in heartfelt prayer, He will answer—in His own time and according to His own plan—and He will do His part to heal us. We, of course, must do our part, too.

And, while we are waiting for God's plans to unfold and for His healing touch to restore us, we can be comforted in the knowledge that our Creator can overcome any obstacle, even if we cannot.

FOOD FOR THOUGHT

What may seem defeat to us may be victory to him.

C. H. Spurgeon

Success or failure can be pretty well predicted by the degree to which the heart is fully in it.

John Eldredge

A HEALTHY-CHOICE TIP

If you're on a new health regimen, you may relapse back into your old, unhealthy habits. If so, don't waste time or energy beating yourself up. If you've "fallen off the wagon," simply pick yourself up, dust yourself off, and get back on it. God was with you when you were riding that wagon the first time, He was with you when you fell, and He'll welcome you back on the wagon when you're wise enough to climb back on.

DAY 62

LASTING PEACE

Be of good comfort, be of one mind, live in peace; and the God of love and peace will be with you.

2 Corinthians 13:11 NKJV

Have you found the lasting peace that can—and should—be yours through Jesus Christ? Or are you still chasing the illusion of "peace and happiness" that the world promises but cannot deliver?

The beautiful words of John 14:27 promise that Jesus offers peace, not as the world gives, but as He alone gives: "Peace I leave with you. My peace I give to you. I do not give to you as the world gives. Your heart must not be troubled or fearful" (HCSB). Your challenge is to accept Christ's peace into your heart and then, as best you can, to share His peace with your neighbors. But sometimes, that's easier said than done.

> God offers peace that passes human understanding . . . and He wants you to make His peace your peace.

If you are a person with lots of obligations and plenty of responsibilities, it is simply a fact of life: You worry. From time to time, you worry about finances, safety, health, home, family, or about countless other concerns, some great and some small. Where is the best place to take your worries? Take them to God . . . and leave them there.

Today, as a gift to yourself, to your family, and to your friends, claim the inner peace that is your spiritual birthright: the peace of Jesus Christ. Christ is standing at the door, waiting patiently for you to invite Him to reign over your heart. His eternal peace is offered freely. Claim it today.

FOOD FOR THOUGHT

The fruit of our placing all things in God's hands is the presence of His abiding peace in our hearts.

Hannah Whitall Smith

I believe that in every time and place it is within our power to acquiesce in the will of God—and what peace it brings to do so!

Elisabeth Elliot

STRENGTHENING YOUR FAITH

Does peace seem to be a distant promise? It is not. God's peace is available to you this very moment if you place absolute trust in Him. Today, let go of your concerns by turning them over to God. Trust Him in the present moment, and accept His peace . . . in the present moment.

MODERATION IS WISDOM IN ACTION

Now if any of you lacks wisdom, he should ask God, who gives to all generously and without criticizing, and it will be given to him.

James 1:5 HCSB

Moderation and wisdom are traveling companions. If we are wise, we must learn to temper our appetites, our desires, and our impulses. When we do, we are blessed, in part, because God has created a world in which temperance is rewarded and intemperance is inevitably punished.

Moderation pays. Excess doesn't. Behave accordingly.

When we allow our appetites to run wild, they usually do. When we abandon moderation, we forfeit the inner peace that God offers—but does not guarantee—to His children. When we live intemperate lives, we rob ourselves of countless blessings that would have otherwise been ours.

God's instructions are clear: if we seek to live wisely, we must be moderate in our appetites and disciplined in our behavior. To do otherwise is an affront to Him . . . and to ourselves.

FOOD FOR THOUGHT

Teach me, O Lord, the way of Your statutes, and I shall keep it to the end.

Psalm 119:33 NKJV

So teach us to number our days, that we may gain a heart of wisdom.

Psalm 90:12 NKJV

Acquire wisdom—how much better it is than gold! And acquire understanding—it is preferable to silver.

Proverbs 16:16 HCSB

A HEALTHY-CHOICE TIP

Of a thousand American adults who were surveyed in a recent poll, eighty-eight percent were unable to accurately estimate how many calories they should consume each day to maintain their weight. Consequently, these adults didn't know how many calories they should consume if they wanted to lose weight. Thankfully, in these days of easy Internet information, it isn't very difficult to discover how many calories you need. So do the research and find your calorie target. Then, aim for the bull's-eye that leads to better health and a longer life.

DAY 64

BEYOND COMPLAINING

Be hospitable to one another without complaining.

1 Peter 4:9 HCSB

Most of us have more blessings than we can count, yet we can still find reasons to complain about the minor frustrations of everyday life. To do so, of course, is not only shortsighted, but it is also a serious roadblock on the path to spiritual abundance.

Would you like to feel more comfortable about your circumstances and your life? Then promise yourself that you'll do whatever it takes to ensure that you focus your thoughts and energy on the major blessings you've received (not the minor inconveniences you must occasionally endure).

If you're wise, you'll fill your heart with gratitude. When you do, there's simply no room left for complaints.

So the next time you're tempted to complain about the inevitable frustrations of everyday living, don't do it! Today and every day, make it a practice to count your blessings, not your hardships. It's the truly decent way to live.

FOOD FOR THOUGHT

It's your choice: you can either count your blessings or recount your disappointments.

Jim Gallery

He wants us to have a faith that does not complain while waiting, but rejoices because we know our times are in His hands—nail-scarred hands that labor for our highest good.

Kay Arthur

I am sure it is never sadness—a proper, straight, natural response to loss—that does people harm, but all the other things, all the resentment, dismay, doubt and self-pity with which it is usually complicated.

C. S. Lewis

When you're on the verge of throwing a pity party thanks to your despairing thoughts, go back to the Word of God.

Charles Swindoll

A HEALTHY-CHOICE TIP

If you're wise, you'll spend more time counting your blessings and less time counting your problems.

FOLLOW YOUR CONSCIENCE

Let us draw near with a true heart in full assurance of faith, our hearts sprinkled clean from an evil conscience and our bodies washed in pure water.

Hebrews 10:22 HCSB

God gave you a conscience for a very good reason: to make your path conform to His will. Billy Graham correctly observed, "Most of us follow our conscience as we follow a wheelbarrow. We push it in front of us in the direction we want to go." To do so, of course, is a profound mistake.

Yet all of us, on occasion, have failed to listen to the voice that God planted in our hearts, and all of us have suffered the consequences.

Listen carefully to your conscience. That little voice inside your head will seldom lead you astray.

Wise believers make it a practice to listen carefully to that quiet internal voice. Count yourself among that number. When your conscience speaks, listen and learn. In all likelihood, God is trying to get His message through. And in all likelihood, it is a message that you desperately need to hear.

FOOD FOR THOUGHT

My conscience is captive to the word of God.

Martin Luther

God desires that we become spiritually healthy enough through faith to have a conscience that rightly interprets the work of the Holy Spirit.

Beth Moore

If I am walking along the street with a very disfiguring hole in the back of my dress, of which I am in ignorance, it is certainly a very great comfort to me to have a kind friend who will tell me of it. And similarly, it is indeed a comfort to know that there is always abiding with me a divine, all-seeing Comforter, who will reprove me for all my faults and will not let me go on in a fatal unconsciousness of them.

Hannah Whitall Smith

A HEALTHY-CHOICE TIP

Here's a time-tested formula for success: have faith in God and do the work. It has been said that there are no shortcuts to any place worth going, and those words apply to your physical fitness, too. There are simply no shortcuts to a healthy lifestyle.

DAY 66

TRUST GOD'S PROMISES

For you need endurance, so that after you have done God's will, you may receive what was promised.

Hebrews 10:36 HCSB

What do you expect from the day ahead? Are you expecting God to do wonderful things, or are you living beneath a cloud of apprehension and doubt? The familiar words of Psalm 118:24 remind us of a profound yet simple truth: "This is the day which the LORD hath made; we will rejoice and be glad in it" (KJV).

God has made many promises to you, and He will keep every single one of them. Your job is to trust God's promises and live accordingly.

For Christian believers, every day begins and ends with God's Son and God's promises. When we accept Christ into our hearts, God promises us the opportunity for earthly peace and spiritual abundance. But more importantly, God promises us the priceless gift of eternal life.

As we face the inevitable challenges of life here on earth, we must arm ourselves with the promises of God's Holy Word. When we do, we can expect the best, not only for the day ahead, but also for all eternity.

FOOD FOR THOUGHT

Our future may look fearfully intimidating, yet we can look up to the Engineer of the Universe, confident that nothing escapes His attention or slips out of the control of those strong hands.

Elisabeth Elliot

Worries carry responsibilities that belong to God, not to you. Worry does not enable us to escape evil; it makes us unfit to cope with it when it comes.

Corrie ten Boom

God will never let you sink under your circumstances. He always provide a safety net and His love always encircles.

Barbara Johnson

Only believe, don't fear. Our Master, Jesus, always watches over us, and no matter what the persecution, Jesus will surely overcome it.

Lottie Moon

STRENGTHENING YOUR FAITH

Of this you can be sure: God's faithfulness is steadfast, unwavering, and eternal.

HE IS SUFFICIENT

And He said to me, "My grace is sufficient for you, for My strength is made perfect in weakness."

2 Corinthians 12:9 NKJV

Of this you can be certain: God is sufficient to meet your needs. Period.

Do the demands of life seem overwhelming at times? If so, you must learn to rely not only upon your own resources, but also upon the promises of your Father in heaven. God will hold your hand and walk with you and your family if you let Him. So even if your circumstances are difficult, trust the Father.

The Psalmist writes, "Weeping may endure for a night, but joy comes in the morning" (Psalm 30:5 NKJV). But when we are suffering, the morning may seem very far away. It is not. God promises that He is "near to those who have a broken heart" (Psalm 34:18 NKJV). When we are troubled, we must turn to Him, and we must encourage our friends and family members to do likewise.

If you'd like infinite protection, there's only one place you can receive it: from an infinite God.

If you are discouraged by the inevitable demands of life here on earth, be mindful of this fact: the loving heart of God is sufficient to meet any challenge . . . including yours.

FOOD FOR THOUGHT

Jesus has been consistently affectionate and true to us. He has shared his great wealth with us. How can we doubt the all-powerful, all-sufficient Lord?

C. H. Spurgeon

God's saints in all ages have realized that God was enough for them. God is enough for time; God is enough for eternity. God is enough!

Hannah Whitall Smith

God will call you to obey Him and do whatever he asks of you. However, you do not need to be doing something to feel fulfilled. You are fulfilled completely in a relationship with God. When you are filled with Him, what else do you need?

Henry Blackaby and Claude King

Yes, God's grace is always sufficient, and His arms are always open to give it. But, will our arms be open to receive it?

Beth Moore

STRENGTHENING YOUR FAITH

Whatever you need, God can provide. He is always sufficient to meet your needs.

STUDY GOD'S WORD

You will be a good servant of Christ Jesus, nourished by the words of the faith and of the good teaching that you have followed.

1 Timothy 4:6 HCSB

God's Word is unlike any other book. The Bible is a road-map for life here on earth and for life eternal. As Christians, we are called upon to study God's Holy Word, to trust its promises, to follow its commandments, and to share its Good News with the world.

Life is a balancing act, and the Bible can help you stay balanced. So let God's Word guide your path today and every day.

As women who seek to follow in the footsteps of the One from Galilee, we must study the Bible and meditate upon its meaning for our lives. Otherwise, we deprive ourselves of a priceless gift from our Creator. God's Holy Word is, indeed, a transforming, life-changing, one-of-a-kind treasure. And, a passing acquaintance with the Good Book is insufficient for Christians who seek to obey God's Word and to understand His will.

FOOD FOR THOUGHT

I need the spiritual revival that comes from spending quiet time alone with Jesus in prayer and in thoughtful meditation on His Word.

Anne Graham Lotz

God can see clearly no matter how dark or foggy the night is. Trust His Word to guide you safely home.

Lisa Whelchel

The Bible is God's Word to man.

Kay Arthur

Weave the unveiling fabric of God's word through your heart and mind. It will hold strong, even if the rest of life unravels.

Gigi Graham Tchividjian

STRENGTHENING YOUR FAITH

Even if you've been studying the Bible for many years, you've still got lots to learn. Bible study should be a lifelong endeavor; make it your lifelong endeavor.

REBELLION INVITES DISASTER

You must follow the Lord your God and fear Him. You must keep His commands and listen to His voice; you must worship Him and remain faithful to Him.

Deuteronomy 13:4 HCSB

For most of us, it is a daunting thought: one day, perhaps soon, we'll come face to face with our Heavenly Father, and we'll be called to account for our actions here on earth. Our personal histories will certainly not be surprising to God; He already knows everything about us. But the full scope of our activities may be surprising to us: some of us will be pleasantly surprised; others will not be.

Be honest with yourself as you consider ways that you have, in the last few days, disobeyed God. Then, think about specific ways that you can be more obedient in the future.

God's commandments are not offered as helpful hints or timely tips. God's commandments are not suggestions; they are ironclad rules for living, rules that we disobey at our own risk.

The English clergyman Thomas Fuller observed, "He does not believe who does not live according to his beliefs." These words are most certainly true. We may proclaim our beliefs to our hearts' content, but our proclamations will mean nothing—to others or to ourselves—unless we accompany our words with deeds that match. The sermons that we live are far more compelling than the ones we preach.

So today, do whatever you can to ensure that your thoughts and your deeds are pleasing to your Creator. Because you will, at some point in the future, be called to account for your actions. And the future may be sooner than you think.

FOOD FOR THOUGHT

Only he who believes is obedient, and only he who is obedient believes.

Dietrich Bonhoeffer

Obedience is the outward expression of your love of God.

Henry Blackaby

STRENGTHENING YOUR FAITH

Every day of your life, you will be tempted to rebel against God's teachings. Your job, simply put, is to guard your heart against the darkness as you focus on the light.

SMALL STEPS

So we must not get tired of doing good, for we will reap at the
proper time if we don't give up.

Galatians 6:9 HCSB

If you want to become more physically fit, you don't have to make one giant leap. You can start with many small steps, and you should. When it comes to any new exercise regimen, starting slowly and improving gradually is the smart way to do it.

Think of one or two small steps you can take to improve your physical and spiritual health.

Crash diets usually crash. And fitness fads fade. But sensible exercise, when combined with a moderate diet, produces results that last.

So if you're determined to improve the state of your health, remember that consistency is the key. Start slowly, avoid injury, be consistent, and expect gradual improvement, not instant success.

FOOD FOR THOUGHT

Do you not know that the runners in a stadium all race, but only one receives the prize? Run in such a way that you may win. Now everyone who competes exercises self-control in everything. However, they do it to receive a perishable crown, but we an imperishable one.

1 Corinthians 9:24-25 HCSB

It is better to finish something than to start it. It is better to be patient than to be proud.

Ecclesiastes 7:8 NCV

Battles are won in the trenches, in the grit and grime of courageous determination; they are won day by day in the arena of life.

Charles Swindoll

By perseverance the snail reached the ark.

C. H. Spurgeon

A HEALTHY-CHOICE TIP

Becoming fit and staying fit is an exercise in perseverance. If you give up at the first sign of trouble, you won't accomplish much. But if you don't give up, you'll eventually improve your health and your life.

ENTRUSTING YOUR HOPES TO GOD

You, Lord, give true peace to those who depend on you, because they trust you.

Isaiah 26:3 NCV

Have you ever felt hope for the future slipping away? If so, you have temporarily lost sight of the hope that we, as believers, must place in the promises of our Heavenly Father. If you are feeling discouraged, worried, or worse, remember the words of Psalm 31: "Be of good courage, and He shall strengthen your heart."

Since God has promised to guide and protect you—now and forever—you should never lose hope.

Because we are saved by a risen Christ, we can have hope for the future, no matter how desperate our circumstances may seem. After all, God has promised that we are His throughout eternity. And, He has told us that we must place our hopes in Him.

Of course, we will face disappointments and failures, but these are only temporary defeats. Of course, this world can be a place of trials and tribulations, but we are secure. God has promised us peace, joy, and eternal life. And God keeps His promises today, tomorrow, and forever.

FOOD FOR THOUGHT

I discovered that sorrow was not to be feared but rather endured with hope and expectancy that God would use it to visit and bless my life.

Jill Briscoe

Never yield to gloomy anticipation. Place your hope and confidence in God. He has no record of failure.

Mrs. Charles E. Cowman

The best we can hope for in this life is a knothole peek at the shining realities ahead. Yet a glimpse is enough. It's enough to convince our hearts that whatever sufferings and sorrows currently assail us aren't worthy of comparison to that which waits over the horizon.

Joni Eareckson Tada

A HEALTHY-CHOICE TIP

If you genuinely want to exercise more, find exercise that you enjoy. And if you can't seem to find exercise that you enjoy, search for ways to make your current exercise program a little less painful and a little more fun.

ACCEPTING GOD'S CALLING

But as God has distributed to each one, as the Lord has called each one, so let him walk.

1 Corinthians 7:17 NKJV

God is calling you to follow a specific path that He has chosen for your life. And it is vitally important that you heed that call. Otherwise, your talents and opportunities may go unused.

Have you already heard God's call? And are you pursuing it with vigor? If so, you're both fortunate and wise. But if you have not yet discovered what God intends for you to do with your life, keep searching and keep praying until you discover why the Creator put you here.

> God has a plan for your life, a divine calling that you can either answer or ignore. Your choice to respond to it will determine the direction you take and the contributions you make.

Remember: God has important work for you to do—work that no one else on earth can accomplish but you. The Creator has placed you in a particular location, amid particular people, with unique opportunities to serve. And He has given you all the tools you need to succeed. So listen for His voice, watch for His signs, and prepare yourself for the call that is sure to come.

FOOD FOR THOUGHT

God never calls without enabling us. In other words, if he calls you to do something, he makes it possible for you to do it.

Luci Swindoll

When you become consumed by God's call on your life, everything will take on new meaning and significance. You will begin to see every facet of your life, including your pain, as a means through which God can work to bring others to Himself.

Charles Stanley

If God has called you, do not spend time looking over your shoulder to see who is following you.

Corrie ten Boom

A HEALTHY-CHOICE TIP

If someone else is cooking your meals, ask that person to help you plan a healthier diet. Without the cooperation of the person who cooks your food, you'll have an incredibly difficult time sticking to a healthier diet.

THE GOOD NEWS

Grace to you and peace from God our Father and the Lord Jesus Christ.

Philippians 1:2 HCSB

God's grace is not earned . . . thank goodness! To earn God's love and His gift of eternal life would be far beyond the abilities of even the most righteous man or woman. Thankfully, grace is not an earthly reward for righteous behavior; it is a blessed spiritual gift which can be accepted by believers who dedicate themselves to God through Christ. When we accept Christ into our hearts, we are saved by His grace.

> God's grace isn't earned, but freely given—what an amazing, humbling gift.

The familiar words of Ephesians 2:8 make God's promise perfectly clear: It is by grace we have been saved, through faith. We are saved not because of our good deeds but because of our faith in Christ.

God's grace is the ultimate gift, and we owe to Him the ultimate in thanksgiving. Let us praise the Creator for His priceless gift, and let us share the Good News with all who cross our paths. We return our Father's love by accepting His grace and by sharing His message and His love. When we do, we are eternally blessed . . . and the Father smiles.

FOOD FOR THOUGHT

God forgets the past. Imitate him.

Max Lucado

I believe that forgiveness can become a continuing cycle: because God forgives us, we're to forgive others; because we forgive others, God forgives us. Scripture presents both parts of the cycle.

Shirley Dobson

God does what few men can do—forgets the sins of others.

Anonymous

Forgiveness is God's command.

Martin Luther

A HEALTHY-CHOICE TIP

Physical fitness is not the result of a single decision that is made "once and for all." Physical fitness results from thousands of decisions that are made day after day, week after week, and year after year.

DAY 74

LEARNING WHEN TO SAY NO

So let us run the race that is before us and never give up. We should remove from our lives anything that would get in the way and the sin that so easily holds us back.

Hebrews 12:1 NCV

You live in a busy world, a world where many folks may be making demands upon your time. If you're like most women, you've got plenty of people pulling you in lots of directions, starting, of course, with your family—but not ending there.

You have a right to say no. Don't feel guilty about asserting that right. When your conscience says no, then you must say it, too.

Perhaps you also have additional responsibilities at work or at church. Maybe you're active in community affairs, or maybe you're involved in any of a hundred other activities that gobble up big portions of your day. If so, you'll need to be sure that you know when to say enough is enough.

When it comes to squeezing more and more obligations onto your daily to-do list, you have the right to say no when you simply don't have the time, the energy, or the desire to do the job. And if you're wise, you'll learn so say no as often as necessary . . . or else!

FOOD FOR THOUGHT

Prescription for a happier and healthier life: resolve to slow down your pace; learn to say no gracefully; resist the temptation to chase after more pleasure, more hobbies, and more social entanglements.

James Dobson

Judge everything in the light of Jesus Christ.

Oswald Chambers

Life is built on character, but character is built on decisions.

Warren Wiersbe

Great relief and satisfaction can come from seeking God's priorities for us in each season, discerning what is "best" in the midst of many noble opportunities, and pouring our most excellent energies into those things.

Beth Moore

A HEALTHY-CHOICE TIP

Remember that you have a right to say "No" to requests that you consider unreasonable or inconvenient. Don't feel guilty for asserting your right to say "No," and don't feel compelled to fabricate excuses for your decisions.

THE GIFT OF LIFE

What a gift life is to those who stay the course! You've heard, of course, of Job's staying power, and you know how God brought it all together for him at the end. That's because God cares, cares right down to the last detail.

James 5:11 MSG

Life is a glorious gift from God. Treat it that way.

This day, like every other, is filled to the brim with opportunities, challenges, and choices. But, no choice that you make is more important than the choice you make concerning God. Today, you will either place Him at the center of your life—or not—and the consequences of that choice have implications that are both temporal and eternal.

Your life is a priceless opportunity, a gift of incalculable worth. You should thank God for the gift of life . . . and you should use that gift wisely.

Sometimes, we don't intentionally neglect God; we simply allow ourselves to become overwhelmed with the demands of everyday life. And then, without our even realizing it, we gradually drift away from the One we need most. Thankfully, God never drifts away from us. He remains always present, always steadfast, always loving.

As you begin this day, place God and His Son where they belong: in your head, in your prayers, on your lips, and in your heart. And then, with God as your guide and companion, let the journey begin.

FOOD FOR THOUGHT

Jesus wants Life for us, Life with a capital L.

John Eldredge

You have a glorious future in Christ! Live every moment in His power and love.

Vonette Bright

Our Lord is the Bread of Life. His proportions are perfect. There never was too much or too little of anything about Him. Feed on Him for a well-balanced ration. All the vitamins and calories are there.

Vance Havner

STRENGTHENING YOUR FAITH

Life is a priceless gift from God. Spend time each day thanking God for His gift.

THE SOURCE OF STRENGTH

And He said to me, "My grace is sufficient for you, for My strength is made perfect in weakness."

2 Corinthians 12:9 NKJV

Where do you go to find strength? The gym? The health food store? The espresso bar? There's a better source of strength, of course, and that source is God. He is a never-ending source of strength and courage if you call upon Him.

Today, think about ways that you can tap into God's strength: try prayer, worship, and praise, for starters.

Are you an energized Christian? You should be. But if you're not, you must seek strength and renewal from the source that will never fail: that source, of course, is your Heavenly Father. And rest assured—when you sincerely petition Him, He will give you all the strength you need to live victoriously for Him.

Have you "tapped in" to the power of God? Have you turned your life and your heart over to Him, or are you muddling along under your own power? The answer to this question will determine the quality of your life here on earth and the destiny of your life throughout all eternity. So start tapping in—and remember that when it comes to strength, God is the Ultimate Source.

FOOD FOR THOUGHT

The God we seek is a God who is intrinsically righteous and who will be so forever. With His example and His strength, we can share in that righteousness.

Bill Hybels

By ourselves we are not capable of suffering bravely, but the Lord possesses all the strength we lack and will demonstrate His power when we undergo persecution.

Corrie ten Boom

Cast yourself into the arms of God and be very sure that if He wants anything of you, He will fit you for the work and give you strength.

Philip Neri

A HEALTHY-CHOICE TIP

As you petition God each morning, ask Him for the strength and the wisdom to treat your body as His creation and His "temple." During the day ahead, you will face countless temptations to do otherwise, but with God's help, you can treat your body as the priceless, one-of-a-kind gift that it most certainly is.

BE PATIENT AND TRUST GOD

Be still before the Lord and wait patiently for Him.

Psalm 37:7 NIV

Psalm 37:7 commands us to wait patiently for God. But as busy women in a fast-paced world, many of us find that waiting quietly for God is difficult. Why? Because we are fallible human beings seeking to live according to our own timetables, not God's. In our better moments, we realize that patience is not only a virtue, but it is also a commandment from God.

> When you learn to be more patient with others, you'll make your world—and your heart—a better place.

We human beings are impatient by nature. We know what we want, and we know exactly when we want it: NOW! But, God knows better. He has created a world that unfolds according to His plans, not our own. As believers, we must trust His wisdom and His goodness.

God instructs us to be patient in all things. We must be patient with our families, our friends, and our associates. We must also be patient with our Creator as He unfolds His plan for our lives. And that's as it should be. After all, think about how patient God has been with us.

FOOD FOR THOUGHT

Wisdom always waits for the right time to act, while emotion always pushes for action right now.

Joyce Meyer

How do you wait upon the Lord? First you must learn to sit at His feet and take time to listen to His words.

Kay Arthur

Let me encourage you to continue to wait with faith. God may not perform a miracle, but He is trustworthy to touch you and make you whole where there used to be a hole.

Lisa Whelchel

Waiting is the hardest kind of work, but God knows best, and we may joyfully leave all in His hands.

Lottie Moon

A HEALTHY-CHOICE TIP

Every step of your life's journey is a choice . . . and the quality of those choices determines the quality of the journey.

CONTAGIOUS CHRISTIANITY

We are therefore Christ's ambassadors, as though God were making his appeal through us. We implore you on Christ's behalf: Be reconciled to God.

2 Corinthians 5:20 NIV

Genuine, heartfelt Christianity can be highly contagious. When you've experienced the transforming power of God's love, you feel the need to share the Good News of His only begotten Son. So, whether you realize it or not, you can be sure that you are being led to share the story of your faith with family, with friends, and with the world.

Every believer, including you, bears responsibility for sharing God's Good News. And it is important to remember that you share your testimony through words and actions, but not necessarily in that order.

Today, don't be bashful or timid: Talk about Jesus and, while you're at it, show the world what it really means to follow Him. After all, the fields are ripe for the harvest, time is short, and the workers are surprisingly few. So please share your story today because tomorrow may indeed be too late.

If you want to be more like Jesus . . . follow in His footsteps every day, obey His commandments every day, and share His never-ending love every day.

FOOD FOR THOUGHT

It has been the faith of the Son of God who loves me and gave Himself for me that has held me in the darkest valley and the hottest fires and the deepest waters.

Elisabeth Elliot

Live your lives in love, the same sort of love which Christ gives us, and which He perfectly expressed when He gave Himself as a sacrifice to God.

Corrie ten Boom

This hard place in which you perhaps find yourself is the very place in which God is giving you opportunity to look only to Him, to spend time in prayer, and to learn long-suffering, gentleness, meekness—in short, to learn the depths of the love that Christ Himself has poured out on all of us.

Elisabeth Elliot

A HEALTHY-CHOICE TIP

Take a careful look inside your refrigerator. Are the contents reflective of a healthy lifestyle? And if your fridge is overflowing with junk foods, it's time to rethink your shopping habits.

GET INVOLVED
IN A CHURCH

And I also say to you that you are Peter, and on this rock I will build My church, and the forces of Hades will not overpower it. I will give you the keys of the kingdom of heaven, and whatever you bind on earth will have been bound in heaven, and whatever you loose on earth will have been loosed in heaven.

Matthew 16:18-19 HCSB

If you want to find balance, the church is a wonderful place to discover it.

Are you an active, contributing, member of your local fellowship? The answer to this simple question will have a profound impact on the direction of your spiritual journey and the content of your character.

> God intends for you to be actively involved in His church. Your intentions should be the same.

If you are not currently engaged in a local church, you're missing out on an array of blessings that include, but are certainly not limited to, the life-lifting relationships that you can—and should—be experiencing with fellow believers.

So do yourself a favor: Find a congregation you're comfortable with, and join it. And once you've joined, don't just attend church out of habit. Go to church out of a sincere desire to know and worship God. When you do, you'll be blessed by the men and women who attend your fellowship, and you'll be blessed by your Creator. You deserve to attend church, and God deserves for you to attend church, so don't delay.

FOOD FOR THOUGHT

Every time a new person comes to God, every time someone's gifts find expression in the fellowship of believers, every time a family in need is surrounded by the caring church, the truth is affirmed anew: the Church triumphant is alive and well!

Gloria Gaither

In God's economy you will be hard-pressed to find many examples of successful "Lone Rangers."

Luci Swindoll

STRENGTHENING YOUR FAITH

Make church a celebration, not an obligation: What you put into church determines what you get out of it. Your attitude towards worship is vitally important . . . so celebrate accordingly!

DURING DIFFICULT DAYS

We also have joy with our troubles, because we know that these troubles produce patience. And patience produces character, and character produces hope.

Romans 5:3-4 NCV

All of us face those occasional days when the traffic jams and the dog gobbles the homework. But, when we find ourselves overtaken by the minor frustrations of life, we must catch ourselves, take a deep breath, and lift our thoughts upward. Although we are here on earth struggling to rise above the distractions of the day, we need never struggle alone. God is here—eternally and faithfully, with infinite patience and love—and, if we reach out to Him, He will restore perspective and peace to our souls.

> Difficult days come and go. Stay the course. The sun is shining somewhere, and will soon shine on you.

Sometimes even the most devout Christians can become discouraged, and you are no exception. After all, you live in a world where expectations can be high and demands can be even higher.

If you find yourself enduring difficult circumstances, remember that God remains in His heaven. If you become discouraged with the direction of your day or your life, lift your thoughts and prayers to Him. He is a God of possibility, not negativity. He will guide you through your difficulties and beyond them. Then, you can thank the Giver of all things good for blessings that are simply too numerous to count.

FOOD FOR THOUGHT

Are you weak? Weary? Confused? Troubled? Pressured? How is your relationship with God? Is it held in its place of priority? I believe the greater the pressure, the greater your need for time alone with Him.

Kay Arthur

The strengthening of faith comes from staying with it in the hour of trial. We should not shrink from tests of faith.

Catherine Marshall

A HEALTHY-CHOICE TIP

Many of the messages that you receive from the media are specifically designed to sell you products that interfere with your spiritual, physical, or emotional health. God takes great interest in your health; the moguls from Madison Avenue take great interest in your pocketbook. Trust God.

THE POWER OF OPTIMISM

I am able to do all things through Him who strengthens me.

Philippians 4:13 HCSB

As each day unfolds, you are quite literally surrounded by more opportunities than you can count—opportunities to improve your own life and the lives of those you love. God's Word promises that you, like all of His children, possess the ability to experience earthly peace and spiritual abundance. Yet sometimes—especially if you dwell upon the inevitable disappointments that may, at times, befall even the luckiest among us—you may allow pessimism to invade your thoughts and your heart.

Be a realistic optimist. Think realistically about yourself and your situation while making a conscious effort to focus on hopes, not fears.

The self-fulfilling prophecy is alive, well, and living at your house. If you constantly anticipate the worst, that's what you're likely to attract. But, if you make the effort to think positive thoughts, you'll increase the probability that those positive thoughts will come true.

So here's a simple, character-building tip for improving your life: put the self-fulfilling prophecy to work for you. Expect the best, and then get busy working to achieve it.

When you do, you'll not only increase the odds of achieving your dreams, but you'll also have more fun along the way.

FOOD FOR THOUGHT

The popular idea of faith is of a certain obstinate optimism: the hope, tenaciously held in the face of trouble, that the universe is fundamentally friendly and things may get better.

J. I. Packer

It is a remarkable thing that some of the most optimistic and enthusiastic people you will meet are those who have been through intense suffering.

Warren Wiersbe

Christ can put a spring in your step and a thrill in your heart. Optimism and cheerfulness are products of knowing Christ.

Billy Graham

A HEALTHY-CHOICE TIP

Learn to look for opportunities, not obstructions; and while you're at it, look for possibilities, not problems.

ACCEPTING LIFE

Do not remember the past events, pay no attention to things of old. Look, I am about to do something new; even now it is coming. Do you not see it? Indeed, I will make a way in the wilderness, rivers in the desert.

Isaiah 43:18-19 HCSB

If you're like most people, you like being in control. Period. When you're trying to improve your health—or any other aspect of your life, for that matter—you want things to happen in accordance with your own specific timetable.

But sometimes, God has other plans . . . and He always has the final word.

Think of at least one aspect of your life that you've been reluctant to accept, and then prayerfully ask God to help you trust Him more by accepting the past.

All of us experience adversity and pain. As human beings with limited comprehension, we can never fully understand the will of our Father in Heaven. But as believers in a benevolent God, we must always trust His providence.

When Jesus went to the Mount of Olives, as described in Luke 22, He poured out His heart to God. Jesus knew of the agony that He was destined to endure, but He also knew that God's will must be done. We, like our Savior, face trials that bring fear and trembling to the very depths of our souls, but like Christ, we too must ultimately seek God's will, not our own.

Are you embittered by a personal tragedy that you did not deserve and cannot understand? If so, it's time to make peace with life. It's time to forgive others, and, if necessary, to forgive yourself. It's time to accept the unchangeable past, to embrace the priceless present, and to have faith in the promise of tomorrow. It's time to trust God completely. And it's time to reclaim the peace—His peace—that can and should be yours.

FOOD FOR THOUGHT

What cannot be altered must be borne, not blamed.

Thomas Fuller

Prayer may not get us what we want, but it will teach us to want what we need.

Vance Havner

A HEALTHY-CHOICE TIP

Are you chained to a desk or trapped in a sedentary lifestyle? And are you waiting for something big to happen before you revolutionize your exercise habits? If so, wait no more. In fact, you can start today by substituting a light snack and a healthy walk for that calorie-laden lunch.

CONSIDER THE POSSIBILITIES

But Jesus looked at them and said, "With men this is impossible, but with God all things are possible."

Matthew 19:26 HCSB

All of us face difficult days. Sometimes even the most optimistic women can become discouraged, and you are no exception. If you find yourself enduring difficult circumstances, perhaps it's time for an extreme intellectual makeover—perhaps it's time to focus more on your strengths and opportunities, and less on the challenges that confront you. And one more thing: perhaps it's time to put a little more faith in God.

Don't invest large quantities of your life focusing on past misfortunes. On the road of life, regret is a dead end.

Every day, including this one, is brimming with possibilities. Every day is filled opportunities to grow, to serve, and to share. But if you are entangled in a web of negativity, you may overlook the blessings that God has scattered along your path. So don't give in to pessimism, to doubt, or to cynicism. Instead, keep your eyes upon the possibilities, fix your heart upon the Creator, do your best, and let Him handle the rest.

FOOD FOR THOUGHT

Here lies the tremendous mystery—that God should be all-powerful, yet refuse to coerce. He summons us to cooperation. We are honored in being given the opportunity to participate in His good deeds. Remember how He asked for help in performing His miracles: Fill the water pots, stretch out your hand, distribute the loaves.

Elisabeth Elliot

God specializes in things fresh and firsthand. His plans for you this year may outshine those of the past. He's prepared to fill your days with reasons to give Him praise.

Joni Eareckson Tada

I could go through this day oblivious to the miracles all around me or I could tune in and "enjoy."

Gloria Gaither

A HEALTHY-CHOICE TIP

The cure for obesity is simple, but implementing that cure isn't. Weight loss requires lots of planning and lots of self-discipline. But with God's help, you're up to the task.

NEW BEGINNINGS

Then the One seated on the throne said, "Look! I am making everything new."

Revelation 21:5 HCSB

Each new day offers countless opportunities to serve God, to seek His will, and to obey His teachings. But each day also offers countless opportunities to stray from God's commandments and to wander far from His path.

Sometimes, we wander aimlessly in a wilderness of our own making, but God has better plans for us. And, whenever we ask Him to renew our strength and guide our steps, He does so.

Consider this day a new beginning. Consider it a fresh start, a renewed opportunity to serve your Creator with willing hands and a loving heart. Ask God to renew your sense of purpose as He guides your steps. Today is a glorious opportunity to serve God. Seize that opportunity while you can; tomorrow may indeed be too late.

If you're graduating into a new phase of life, be sure to make God your partner. If you do, He'll guide your steps, He'll help carry your burdens, and He'll help you focus on the things that really matter.

FOOD FOR THOUGHT

Whoever you are, whatever your condition or circumstance, whatever your past or problem, Jesus can restore you to wholeness.

Anne Graham Lotz

Walking with God leads to receiving his intimate counsel, and counseling leads to deep restoration.

John Eldredge

God is not running an antique shop! He is making all things new!

Vance Havner

The amazing thing about Jesus is that He doesn't just patch up our lives, He gives us a brand new sheet, a clean slate to start over, all new.

Gloria Gaither

STRENGTHENING YOUR FAITH

How do you know if you can still keep growing as a Christian? Check your pulse. If it's still beating, then you can still keep growing.

MOVING MOUNTAINS

If you have faith as a mustard seed, you will say to this mountain, "Move from here to there," and it will move; and nothing will be impossible for you.

Matthew 17:20 NKJV

Every life—including yours—is a series of successes and failures, celebrations and disappointments, joys and sorrows. Every step of the way, through every triumph and tragedy, God will stand by your side and strengthen you . . . if you have faith in Him. Jesus taught His disciples that if they had faith, they could move mountains. You can too.

> The quality of your faith will help determine the quality of your day and the quality of your life.

When a suffering woman sought healing by merely touching the hem of His cloak, Jesus replied, "Daughter, be of good comfort; thy faith hath made thee whole" (Matthew 9:22 KJV). The message to believers of every generation is clear: we must live by faith today and every day.

When you place your faith, your trust, indeed your life in the hands of Christ Jesus, you'll be amazed at the marvelous things He can do with you and through you. So strengthen your faith through praise, through worship, through Bible study, and through prayer. And trust God's plans. With Him, all things are possible, and He stands ready to open a world of possibilities to you . . . if you have faith.

FOOD FOR THOUGHT

Faith is seeing light with the eyes of your heart, when the eyes of your body see only darkness.

Barbara Johnson

Grace calls you to get up, throw off your blanket of helplessness, and to move on through life in faith.

Kay Arthur

Just as our faith strengthens our prayer life, so do our prayers deepen our faith. Let us pray often, starting today, for a deeper, more powerful faith.

Shirley Dobson

STRENGTHENING YOUR FAITH

If you don't have faith, you'll never move mountains. But if you do have faith, there's no limit to the things that you and God, working together, can accomplish.

LIVE ON PURPOSE

I, therefore, the prisoner in the Lord, urge you to walk worthy of the calling you have received.

Ephesians 4:1 HCSB

"What on earth does God intend for me to do with my life?" It's an easy question to ask but, for many of us, a difficult question to answer. Why? Because God's purposes aren't always clear to us. Sometimes we wander aimlessly in a wilderness of our own making. And sometimes, we struggle mightily against God in an unsuccessful attempt to find success and happiness through our own means, not His.

God has a plan for your life, a definite purpose that you can fulfill. Your challenge is to pray for God's guidance and to follow wherever He leads.

If you're a woman who sincerely seeks God's guidance, He will give it. But, He will make His revelations known to you in a way and in a time of His choosing, not yours, so be patient. If you prayerfully petition God and work diligently to discern His intentions, He will, in time, lead you to a place of joyful abundance and eternal peace.

Sometimes, God's intentions will be clear to you; other times, God's plan will seem uncertain at best. But even on those difficult days when your life seems dangerously out of balance, you must never lose sight of these overriding facts: God created you for a reason; He has important work for you to do; and He's waiting patiently for you to do it. The next step is up to you.

FOOD FOR THOUGHT

Only God's chosen task for you will ultimately satisfy. Do not wait until it is too late to realize the privilege of serving Him in His chosen position for you.

Beth Moore

His life is our light—our purpose and meaning and reason for living.

Anne Graham Lotz

Yesterday is just experience but tomorrow is glistening with purpose—and today is the channel leading from one to the other.

Barbara Johnson

A HEALTHY-CHOICE TIP

God's Word is full of advice about health, moderation, and sensible living. When you come across these passages, take them to heart and put them to use.

SAFETY FIRST

The sensible see danger and take cover; the foolish keep going and are punished.

Proverbs 27:12 HCSB

We live in a world that can be a dangerous place, especially for those who are inclined toward risky behaviors. Some risk takers are easy to spot: they jump out of little airplanes, scurry up tall mountains, or race very fast automobiles.

Most risk takers, however, are not so bold; instead, they take more subtle risks that endanger themselves, their friends, and their families. They drink and drive, or they smoke cigarettes, or they neglect to fasten their seatbelts, or they engage in countless other behaviors that, while not as glamorous as mountain climbing, are equally as dangerous.

Put the brakes on risky behaviors . . . before risky behaviors put the brakes on you.

This world holds enough hazards of its own without our adding to those risks by foolishly neglecting our own personal safety and the safety of those around us. So, the next time you're tempted to do something foolish, remember that the body you're putting at risk belongs not only to you, but also to God. And He hopes that you'll behave wisely.

FOOD FOR THOUGHT

Sometimes, being wise is nothing more than slowing down long enough to think about things before you do them.

Jim Gallery

If we neglect the Bible, we cannot expect to benefit from the wisdom and direction that result from knowing God's Word.

Vonette Bright

Wisdom is knowledge applied. Head knowledge is useless on the battlefield. Knowledge stamped on the heart makes one wise.

Beth Moore

The more wisdom enters our hearts, the more we will be able to trust our hearts in difficult situations.

John Eldredge

A HEALTHY-CHOICE TIP

Remember: life is God's gift to you—taking good care of yourself is your gift to God.

YOU DON'T HAVE
TO BE PERFECT

To acquire wisdom is to love oneself; people who cherish understanding will prosper.

Proverbs 19:8 NLT

You don't have to be perfect to be wonderful. The difference between perfectionism and realistic expectations is the difference between a life of frustration and a life of contentment. Only one earthly being ever lived life to perfection, and He was the Son of God. The rest of us have fallen short of God's standard and need to be accepting of our own limitations as well as the limitations of others.

If you find yourself frustrated by the unrealistic demands of others (or by unrealistic pressures of the self-imposed variety) it's time to ask yourself who you're trying to impress, and why. Your first responsibility is to the Heavenly Father who created you and to the Son who saved you. Then, you bear a powerful responsibility to be true to yourself. And of course you owe debts of gratitude to friends and family members. But, when it comes to meeting society's unrealistic expectations, forget it! Those expectations aren't just unrealistic; they're detrimental to your spiritual health.

So, if you've become discouraged with your inability to be perfectly fit, remember that when you accepted

Christ as your Savior, God accepted you for all eternity. Now, it's your turn to accept yourself. When you do, you'll feel a tremendous weight being lifted from your shoulders. After all, pleasing God is simply a matter of obeying His commandments and accepting His Son. But as for pleasing everybody else? That's impossible . . . so why even try?

FOOD FOR THOUGHT

A perfectionist resists the truth that growing up in Christ is a process.

Susan Lenzkes

STRENGTHENING YOUR FAITH

As you begin to work toward improved physical and emotional health, don't expect perfection. Of course you should work hard; of course you should be disciplined; of course you should do your best. But then, when you've given it your best effort, you should be accepting of yourself, imperfect though you may be. In heaven, we will know perfection. Here on earth, we have a few short years to wrestle with the challenges of imperfection. Let us accept these lives that God has given us—and these bodies which are ours for a brief time here on earth—with open, loving arms.

TOO FRIENDLY WITH THE WORLD?

Let no one deceive himself. If anyone among you seems to be wise in this age, let him become a fool that he may become wise. For the wisdom of this world is foolishness with God. For it is written, "He catches the wise in their own craftiness."

1 Corinthians 3:18–19 NKJV

We live in the world, but we should not worship it—yet at every turn, or so it seems, we are tempted to do otherwise. As Warren Wiersbe correctly observed, "Because the world is deceptive, it is dangerous."

The world makes plenty of promises that it can't keep. God, on the other hand, keeps every single one of His promises.

The 21st-century world in which we live is a noisy, distracting place, a place that offers countless temptations and dangers. The world seems to cry, "Worship me with your time, your money, your energy, your thoughts, and your life!" But if we are wise, we won't fall prey to that temptation.

If you wish to build your character day-by-day, you must distance yourself, at least in part, from the temptations and distractions of modern-day society. But distancing yourself isn't easy, especially when so many societal forces are struggling to capture your attention, your participation, and your money.

C. S. Lewis said, "Aim at heaven and you will get earth thrown in; aim at earth and you will get neither." That's good advice. You're likely to hit what you aim at, so aim high . . . aim at heaven. When you do, you'll be strengthening your character as you improve every aspect of your life. And God will demonstrate His approval as He showers you with more spiritual blessings than you can count.

FOOD FOR THOUGHT

The more we stuff ourselves with material pleasures, the less we seem to appreciate life.

Barbara Johnson

A HEALTHY-CHOICE TIP

In the good old days, dining out used to be an occasional treat for most families. Now, it's more of an everyday occurrence. But there's a catch: most restaurants aim for taste first, price second, and health a distant third. But you should think health first. So the next time you head out for a burger, a bagel, or any other fast food, take a minute to read the fine print that's usually posted on the wall. You may find out that the healthy-sounding treat is actually a calorie-bomb in disguise.

GETTING ENOUGH REST?

Come to Me, all you who labor and are heavy laden, and I will give you rest. Take My yoke upon you and learn from Me, for I am gentle and lowly in heart, and you will find rest for your souls. For My yoke is easy and My burden is light.

Matthew 11:28-30 NKJV

Even the most inspired Christians can, from time to time, find themselves running on empty. The demands of daily life can drain us of our strength and rob us of the joy that is rightfully ours in Christ. When we find ourselves tired, discouraged, or worse, there is a source from which we can draw the power needed to recharge our spiritual batteries. That source is God.

God wants you to get enough rest. The world wants you to burn the candle at both ends. Trust God.

God intends that His children lead joyous lives filled with abundance and peace. But sometimes, abundance and peace seem very far away. It is then that we must turn to God for renewal, and when we do, He will restore us.

God expects us to work hard, but He also intends for us to rest. When we fail to take the rest that we need, we do a disservice to ourselves and to our families.

Is your spiritual battery running low? Is your energy on the wane? Are your emotions frayed? If so, it's time to turn your thoughts and your prayers to God. And when you're finished, it's time to rest.

FOOD FOR THOUGHT

Satan does some of his worst work on exhausted Christians when nerves are frayed and their minds are faint.

Vance Havner

Jesus taught us by example to get out of the rat race and recharge our batteries.

Barbara Johnson

Life is strenuous. See that your clock does not run down.

Mrs. Charles E. Cowman

A HEALTHY-CHOICE TIP

You live in a world that tempts you to stay up late—very late. But too much late-night TV, combined with too little sleep, is a prescription for exhaustion, ill health, ill temper, or all three. So do yourself, your boss, and your loved ones a big favor. Arrange your TV schedule and your life so you get eight hours of sleep every night.

MAKING GOD'S PRIORITIES YOUR PRIORITIES

Draw near to God, and He will draw near to you.

James 4:8 HCSB

Have you fervently asked God to help prioritize your life? Have you asked Him for guidance and for the courage to do the things that you know need to be done? If so, then you're continually inviting your Creator to reveal Himself in a variety of ways. As a follower of Christ, you must do no less.

> The priorities you choose will dictate the life you live. So choose carefully. And don't be afraid to say no when you begin to feel overcommitted.

When you make God's priorities your priorities, you will receive God's abundance and His peace. When you make God a full partner in every aspect of your life, He will help you keep things in balance. When you allow God to reign over your heart, He will honor you with spiritual blessings that are simply too numerous to count. So, as you plan for the day ahead, make God's will your ultimate priority. When you do, every other priority will have a tendency to fall neatly into place.

FOOD FOR THOUGHT

Blessed are those who know what on earth they are here on earth to do and set themselves about the business of doing it.

Max Lucado

The essence of the Christian life is Jesus: that in all things He might have the preeminence, not that in some things He might have a place.

Franklin Graham

How important it is for us—young and old—to live as if Jesus would return any day—to set our goals, make our choices, raise our children, and conduct business with the perspective of the imminent return of our Lord.

Gloria Gaither

A HEALTHY-CHOICE TIP

Simply put, it's up to you to assume the ultimate responsibility for your health. So if you're fighting the battle of the bulge (the bulging waistline, that is), don't waste your time blaming the fast food industry—or anybody else, for that matter. It's your body, and it's your responsibility to take care of it.

PAYING ATTENTION TO GOD

For where your treasure is, there your heart will be also.

Luke 12:34 HCSB

Who is in charge of your heart? Is it God, or is it something else? Have you given Christ your heart, your soul, your talents, your time, and your testimony? Or are you giving Him little more than a few hours each Sunday morning?

In the book of Exodus, God warns that we should place no gods before Him. Yet all too often, we place our Lord in second, third, or fourth place as we worship other things. When we unwittingly place possessions or relationships above our love for the Creator, we create big problems for ourselves.

Because God is infinite and eternal, you cannot comprehend Him. But you can understand your need to praise Him, to love Him, and to obey His Word.

Does God rule your heart? Make certain that the honest answer to this question is a resounding yes. In the life of every Christian, God should come first. And that's precisely the place that He deserves in your heart.

FOOD FOR THOUGHT

In heaven, we will see that nothing, absolutely nothing, was wasted, and that every tear counted and every cry was heard.

Joni Eareckson Tada

God loves each of us as if there were only one of us.

St. Augustine

He treats us as sons, and all he asks in return is that we shall treat Him as a Father whom we can trust without anxiety. We must take the son's place of dependence and trust, and we must let Him keep the father's place of care and responsibility.

Hannah Whitall Smith

He is always thinking about us. We are before his eyes. The Lord's eye never sleeps, but is always watching out for our welfare. We are continually on his heart.

C. H. Spurgeon

A HEALTHY-CHOICE TIP

Don't worship food. Honor the body that God gave you by eating sensible portions of sensible foods.

SEEK FELLOWSHIP

Then all the people began to eat and drink, send portions, and have a great celebration, because they had understood the words that were explained to them.

Nehemiah 8:12 HCSB

Fellowship with other believers should be an integral part of your everyday life. Your association with fellow Christians should be uplifting, enlightening, encouraging, and consistent.

Are you an active member of your own fellowship? Are you a builder of bridges inside the four walls of your church and outside it? Do you contribute to God's glory by contributing your time and your talents to a close-knit band of believers? Hopefully so. The fellowship of believers is intended to be a powerful tool for spreading God's Good News and uplifting His children. And God intends for you to be a fully contributing member of that fellowship. Your intentions should be the same.

If you're experiencing a strained relationship with someone, take steps to mend that relationship . . . and do it now.

FOOD FOR THOUGHT

In God's economy you will be hard-pressed to find many examples of successful "Lone Rangers."

Luci Swindoll

Christians are like coals of a fire. Together they glow— apart they grow cold.

Anonymous

Be united with other Christians. A wall with loose bricks is not good. The bricks must be cemented together.

Corrie ten Boom

One of the ways God refills us after failure is through the blessing of Christian fellowship. Just experiencing the joy of simple activities shared with other children of God can have a healing effect on us.

Anne Graham Lotz

STRENGTHENING YOUR FAITH

You need fellowship with men and women of faith. And your Christian friends need fellowship with you. So what are you waiting for?

REMEMBER THE SABBATH

Remember the Sabbath day, to keep it holy.

Exodus 20:8 NKJV

When God gave Moses the Ten Commandments, it became perfectly clear that our Heavenly Father intends for us to make the Sabbath a holy day, a day for worship, for contemplation, for fellowship, and for rest. Yet we live in a seven-day-a-week world, a world that all too often treats Sunday as a regular workday.

One way to strengthen your faith is by giving God at least one day each week. If you carve out the time for a day of worship and praise, you'll be amazed at the impact it will have on the rest of your week. But if you fail to honor God's day, if you treat the Sabbath as a day to work or a day to party, you'll miss out on a harvest of blessings that is only available one day each week.

The Sabbath is unlike the other six days of the week, and it's up to you to treat it that way.

How does your family observe the Lord's day? When church is over, do you treat Sunday like any other day of the week? If so, it's time to think long and hard about your family's schedule and your family's priorities. And if you've been treating Sunday as just another day, it's time to break that habit. When Sunday rolls around, don't try to fill every spare moment. Take time to rest . . . Father's orders!

FOOD FOR THOUGHT

Jesus taught us by example to get out of the rat race and recharge our batteries.

Barbara Johnson

Jesus gives us the ultimate rest, the confidence we need, to escape the frustration and chaos of the world around us.

Billy Graham

It is what Jesus is, not what we are, that gives rest to the soul. If we really want to overcome Satan and have peace with God, we must "fix our eyes on Jesus." Let his death, his suffering, his glories, and his intercession be fresh on your mind.

C. H. Spurgeon

STRENGTHENING YOUR FAITH

Working seven days a week may impress your boss . . . but it isn't the way God intends for you to live your life. You live in a world that doesn't often honor the Sabbath, but God wants you to treat the Sabbath as a day of rest, no exceptions. So next Sunday, do yourself and your family a favor: take God at His Word by making the Sabbath a special day for you and your family.

EXPERIENCING SILENCE

Be still, and know that I am God.

Psalm 46:10 NKJV

The world seems to grow louder day by day, and our senses seem to be invaded at every turn. If we allow the distractions of a clamorous society to separate us from God's peace, we do ourselves a profound disservice. Our task, as dutiful believers, is to carve out moments of silence in a world filled with noise.

If we are to maintain righteous minds and compassionate hearts, we must take time each day for prayer and for meditation. We must make ourselves still in the presence of our Creator. We must quiet our minds and our hearts so that we might sense God's will and His love.

> Spend a few moments each day in silence. You owe it to your Creator . . . and to yourself.

Has the busy pace of life robbed you of the peace that God has promised? If so, it's time to reorder your priorities and your life. As you try to balance the priorities on your daily to-do list, remember that nothing is more important than the time you spend with your Heavenly Father. So be still and claim the inner peace that is found in the silent moments you spend with God.

FOOD FOR THOUGHT

It is in that stillness that the Voice will be heard, the only voice in all the universe that speaks peace to the deepest part of us.

Elisabeth Elliot

Let your loneliness be transformed into a holy aloneness. Sit still before the Lord. Remember Naomi's word to Ruth: "Sit still, my daughter, until you see how the matter will fall."

Elisabeth Elliot

Because Jesus Christ is our Great High Priest, not only can we approach God without a human "go-between," we can also hear and learn from God in some sacred moments without one.

Beth Moore

A HEALTHY-CHOICE TIP

If you place a high value on the body God has given you, then place high importance on the foods you use to fuel it.

KEEPING IN BALANCE BY KEEPING IT SIMPLE

But godliness with contentment is a great gain. For we brought nothing into the world, and we can take nothing out. But if we have food and clothing, we will be content with these. But those who want to be rich fall into temptation, a trap, and many foolish and harmful desires, which plunge people into ruin and destruction.

1 Timothy 6:6-9 HCSB

You live in a world where simplicity is in short supply. Think for a moment about the complexity of your everyday life and compare it to the lives of your ancestors. Certainly, you are the beneficiary of many technological innovations, but those innovations have a price: in all likelihood, your world is highly complex. Consider the following:

Simplicity and peace are two concepts that are closely related. Complexity and peace are not.

1. From the moment you wake up in the morning until the time you lay your head on the pillow at night, you are the target of an endless stream of advertising information. Each message is intended to grab your attention in order to convince you to purchase things you didn't know you needed (and probably don't!).

2. Essential aspects of your life, including personal matters such as health care, are subject to an ever-increasing flood of rules and regulations.

3. Unless you take firm control of your time and your life, you may be overwhelmed by the tidal wave of complexity that threatens your happiness.

Your Heavenly Father understands the joy of living simply, and so should you. So do yourself a favor: keep your life as simple as possible. Simplicity is, indeed, genius. By simplifying your life, you are destined to improve it.

FOOD FOR THOUGHT

There is absolutely no evidence that complexity and materialism lead to happiness. On the contrary, there is plenty of evidence that simplicity and spirituality lead to joy, a blessedness that is better than happiness.

Dennis Swanberg

A HEALTHY-CHOICE TIP

If you're in reasonably good shape, a nice healthy walk can be a great substitute for a big sit-down meal. So don't underestimate the benefits of a good walk. It's a great way to burn a few calories, to get some fresh air, and to improve your life.

LIFETIME LEARNING

The wise person makes learning a joy; fools spout only foolishness.

Proverbs 15:2 NLT

When it comes to learning life's lessons, we can either do things the easy way or the hard way. The easy way can be summed up as follows: when God teaches us a lesson, we learn it . . . the first time! Unfortunately, too many of us—both parents and children alike—learn much more slowly than that.

God still has important lessons to teach you. Your task is to be open to His instruction.

When we resist God's instruction, He continues to teach, whether we like it or not. And if we keep making the same old mistakes, God responds by rewarding us with the same old results.

Our challenge, then, is to discern God's lessons from the experiences of everyday life. Hopefully, we learn those lessons sooner rather than later because the sooner we do, the sooner He can move on to the next lesson and the next, and the next . . .

FOOD FOR THOUGHT

True learning can take place at every age of life, and it doesn't have to be in the curriculum plan.

Suzanne Dale Ezell

While chastening is always difficult, if we look to God for the lesson we should learn, we will see spiritual fruit.

Vonette Bright

The wonderful thing about God's schoolroom is that we get to grade our own papers. You see, He doesn't test us so He can learn how well we're doing. He tests us so we can discover how well we're doing.

Charles Swindoll

STRENGTHENING YOUR FAITH

Today is your classroom: what will you learn? Will you use today's experiences as tools for personal, spiritual, and physical improvement, or will you ignore the lessons that life and God are trying to teach you? Will you carefully study God's Word, and will you apply His teachings to the experiences of everyday life? The events of today have much to teach. You have much to learn. May you live—and learn—accordingly.

FITNESS IS A FORM OF WORSHIP

Worship the Lord your God and . . . serve Him only.

Matthew 4:10 HCSB

What does worship have to do with fitness? That depends on how you define worship. If you consider worship to be a "Sunday-only" activity, an activity that occurs only inside the four walls of your local church, then fitness and worship may seem totally unrelated. But, if you view worship as an activity that impacts every facet of your life—if you consider worship to be something far more than a "one-day-a week" obligation—then you understand that every aspect of your life is a form of worship. And that includes keeping your body physically fit.

> When you worship God with a sincere heart, He will guide your steps and bless your life.

Every day provides opportunities to put God where He belongs: at the center of our lives. When we do so, we worship not just with our words, but also with our deeds. And one way that we can honor our Heavenly Father is by treating our bodies with care and respect.

The Bible makes it clear: "Your body is the temple of the Holy Spirit" (1 Corinthians 6:19 NLT). Treat it that way. And consider your fitness regimen to be one way—a very important way—of worshipping God.

FOOD FOR THOUGHT

It's the definition of worship: A hungry heart finding the Father's feast. A searching soul finding the Father's face. A wandering pilgrim spotting the Father's house. Finding God. Finding God seeking us. This is worship. This is a worshiper.

Max Lucado

There is no division into sacred and secular; it is all one great, glorious life.

Oswald Chambers

God asks that we worship Him with our concentrated minds as well as with our wills and emotions. A divided and scattered mind is not effective.

Catherine Marshall

A HEALTHY-CHOICE TIP

Consider your healthy lifestyle a form of worship: When God described your body as a temple, He wasn't kidding. Show your respect for God's Word by keeping your temple in tip-top shape.

YOUR PHYSICAL AND SPIRITUAL FITNESS: WHO'S IN CHARGE?

But seek ye first the kingdom of God, and his righteousness; and all these things shall be added unto you.

Matthew 6:33 KJV

One of the surest ways to improve your health and your life—and the best way—is to do it with God as your partner. When you put God first in every aspect of your life, you'll be comforted by the knowledge that His wisdom is the ultimate wisdom and that His plans are the right plans for you. When you put God first, your outlook will change, your priorities will change, your behaviors will change, and your health will change. When you put Him first, you'll experience the genuine peace and lasting comfort that only He can give.

> God deserves first place in your life . . . and you deserve the experience of putting Him there.

In the book of Exodus, God instructs us to place no gods before Him (20:3). Does God rule your heart? Make certain that the honest answer to this question is a resounding yes. And then prepare yourself for the cascade of spiritual and emotional blessings that are sure to follow.

FOOD FOR THOUGHT

The LORD is my strength and my song; he has become my victory. He is my God, and I will praise him.

Exodus 15:2 NLT

Love the Lord your God with all your heart, with all your soul, and with all your strength.

Deuteronomy 6:5 HCSB

Make God's will the focus of your life day by day. If you seek to please Him and Him alone, you'll find yourself satisfied with life.

Kay Arthur

Jesus Christ is the first and last, author and finisher, beginning and end, alpha and omega, and by Him all other things hold together. He must be first or nothing. God never comes next!

Vance Havner

STRENGTHENING YOUR FAITH

God has a plan for the world and for you. When you discover His plan for your life—and when you follow in the footsteps of His Son—you will be rewarded. The place where God is leading you is the place where you must go.

DAY 100

GIVE HIM YOUR HEART

For God so loved the world that He gave His only begotten Son, that whoever believes in Him should not perish but have everlasting life.

John 3:16 NKJV

Your decision to allow Christ to reign over your heart is the pivotal decision of your life. It is a decision that you cannot ignore. It is a decision that is yours and yours alone.

God's love for you is deeper and more profound than you can imagine. God's love for you is so great that He sent His only Son to this earth to die for your sins and to offer you the priceless gift of eternal life. Now, you must decide whether or not to accept God's gift. Will you ignore it or embrace it? Will you return it or neglect it? Will you accept Christ's love and build a lifelong relationship with Him, or will you turn away from Him and take a different path?

> The ultimate choice for you is the choice to invite God's Son into your heart. Choose wisely . . . and immediately.

Accept God's gift now: allow His Son to preside over your heart, your thoughts, and your life, starting this very instant.

FOOD FOR THOUGHT

Choose Jesus Christ! Deny yourself, take up the Cross, and follow Him—for the world must be shown. The world must see, in us, a discernible, visible, startling difference.

Elisabeth Elliot

The most profound essence of my nature is that I am capable of receiving God.

St. Augustine

It's your heart that Jesus longs for: your will to be made His own with self on the cross forever, and Jesus alone on the throne.

Ruth Bell Graham

The amount of power you experience to live a victorious, triumphant Christian life is directly proportional to the freedom you give the Spirit to be Lord of your life!

Anne Graham Lotz

STRENGTHENING YOUR FAITH

If you've already accepted Christ into your heart, congratulations! If you haven't, the appropriate moment to do so is this one.

MORE FROM GOD'S WORD

Verses by Topic

FAITH

If you do not stand firm in your faith, then you will not stand at all.

Isaiah 7:9 HCSB

Be alert, stand firm in the faith, be brave and strong.

1 Corinthians 16:13 HCSB

For we walk by faith, not by sight.

2 Corinthians 5:7 HCSB

Now faith is the reality of what is hoped for, the proof of what is not seen.

Hebrews 11:1 HCSB

Now without faith it is impossible to please God, for the one who draws near to Him must believe that He exists and rewards those who seek Him.

Hebrews 11:6 HCSB

GOD'S LOVE

For God loved the world in this way: He gave His only Son, so that everyone who believes in Him will not perish but have eternal life.

John 3:16 HCSB

For the Lord is good, and His love is eternal; His faithfulness endures through all generations.

Psalm 100:5 HCSB

The one who has My commandments and keeps them is the one who loves Me. And the one who loves Me will be loved by My Father. I also will love him and will reveal Myself to him.

John 14:21 HCSB

We love Him because He first loved us.

1 John 4:19 NKJV

Draw near to God, and He will draw near to you.

James 4:8 HCSB

WISDOM

Therefore, everyone who hears these words of Mine and acts on them will be like a sensible man who built his house on the rock. The rain fell, the rivers rose, and the winds blew and pounded that house. Yet it didn't collapse, because its foundation was on the rock.

Matthew 7:24–25 HCSB

But from Him you are in Christ Jesus, who for us became wisdom from God, as well as righteousness, sanctification, and redemption.

1 Corinthians 1:30 HCSB

For God has not given us a spirit of fearfulness, but one of power, love, and sound judgment.

2 Timothy 1:7 HCSB

Now if any of you lacks wisdom, he should ask God, who gives to all generously and without criticizing, and it will be given to him.

James 1:5 HCSB

THE SIMPLE LIFE

A simple life in the Fear-of-God is better than a rich life with a ton of headaches.

Proverbs 15:16 MSG

Do not love the world or the things in the world. If anyone loves the world, the love of the Father is not in him.

1 John 2:15 NKJV

We brought nothing into the world, so we can take nothing out. But, if we have food and clothes, we will be satisfied with that.

1 Timothy 6:7-8 NCV

So think clearly and exercise self-control. Look forward to the special blessings that will come to you at the return of Jesus Christ.

1 Peter 1:13 NLT

For the grace of God has been revealed, bringing salvation to all people. And we are instructed to turn from godless living and sinful pleasures. We should live in this evil world with self-control, right conduct, and devotion to God.

Titus 2:11-12 NLT

RIGHTEOUSNESS

The righteous one will live by his faith.

Habakkuk 2:4 HCSB

And the world is passing away, and the lust of it; but he who does the will of God abides forever.

1 John 2:17 NKJV

Because the eyes of the Lord are on the righteous and His ears are open to their request. But the face of the Lord is against those who do evil.

1 Peter 3:12 HCSB

Flee from youthful passions, and pursue righteousness, faith, love, and peace, along with those who call on the Lord from a pure heart.

2 Timothy 2:22 HCSB

And now, Israel, what does the Lord your God ask of you except to fear the Lord your God by walking in all His ways, to love Him, and to worship the Lord your God with all your heart and all your soul?

Deuteronomy 10:12 HCSB

YOUR PRIORITIES

Don't abandon wisdom, and she will watch over you; love her, and she will guard you.

Proverbs 4:6 HCSB

And I pray this: that your love will keep on growing in knowledge and every kind of discernment, so that you can determine what really matters and can be pure and blameless in the day of Christ.

Philippians 1:9 HCSB

So teach us to number our days, that we may gain a heart of wisdom.

Psalm 90:12 NKJV

For where your treasure is, there your heart will be also.

Luke 12:34 HCSB

He said to them all, "If anyone desires to come after Me, let him deny himself, and take up his cross daily, and follow Me. For whoever desires to save his life will lose it, but whoever loses his life for My sake will save it."

Luke 9:23-24 NKJV

ASKING FOR GOD'S HELP

If you remain in Me and My words remain in you, ask whatever you want and it will be done for you.

John 15:7 HCSB

What father among you, if his son asks for a fish, will, instead of a fish, give him a snake? Or if he asks for an egg, will give him a scorpion? If you then, who are evil, know how to give good gifts to your children, how much more will the heavenly Father give the Holy Spirit to those who ask Him?

Luke 11:11-13 HCSB

Don't worry about anything, but in everything, through prayer and petition with thanksgiving, let your requests be made known to God.

Philippians 4:6 HCSB

You do not have because you do not ask.

James 4:2 HCSB

For the Lord gives wisdom; from His mouth come knowledge and understanding.

Proverbs 2:6 NKJV

GOD'S STRENGTH

Be of good courage, and let us be strong for our people and for the cities of our God. And may the Lord do what is good in His sight.

1 Chronicles 19:13 NKJV

Do you not know? Have you not heard? The Everlasting God, the LORD, the Creator of the ends of the earth does not become weary or tired. His understanding is inscrutable. He gives strength to the weary, and to him who lacks might He increases power. Though youths grow weary and tired, and vigorous young men stumble badly, yet those who wait for the LORD will gain new strength; they will mount up with wings like eagles, they will run and not get tired, they will walk and not become weary.

Isaiah 40:28–31 NASB

He said unto me, My grace is sufficient for thee: for my strength is made perfect in weakness.

2 Corinthians 12:9 KJV

The LORD is my strength and my song....

Exodus 15:2 NIV

LIFE

I urge you now to live the life to which God called you.

Ephesians 4:1 NKJV

Shout triumphantly to the Lord, all the earth. Serve the Lord with gladness; come before Him with joyful songs.

Psalm 100:1-2 HCSB

Rejoice in the Lord always. Again I will say, rejoice!

Philippians 4:4 NKJV

Jesus told him, "I am the way, the truth, and the life. No one comes to the Father except through Me."

John 14:6 HCSB

He who follows righteousness and mercy finds life, righteousness and honor.

Proverbs 21:21 NKJV

LIFETIME LEARNING

A wise person pays attention to correction that will improve his life.

Proverbs 15:31 ICB

Remember what you are taught, and listen carefully to words of knowledge.

Proverbs 23:12 NCV

The fear of the Lord is the beginning of knowledge, but fools despise wisdom and discipline.

Proverbs 1:7 NIV

The knowledge of the secrets of the kingdom of heaven has been given to you....

Matthew 13:11 NIV

It is not good to have zeal without knowledge, nor to be hasty and miss the way.

Proverbs 19:2 NIV

SILENCE

Be still, and know that I am God.

Psalm 46:10 NKJV

Be silent before the Lord and wait expectantly for Him.

Psalm 37:7 HCSB

In quietness and confidence shall be your strength.

Isaiah 30:15 NKJV

I am not alone, because the Father is with Me.

John 16:32 HCSB

Draw near to God, and He will draw near to you.

James 4:8 HCSB

VALUES

God's Way is not a matter of mere talk; it's an empowered life.

1 Corinthians 4:20 MSG

Walk in a manner worthy of the God who calls you into His own kingdom and glory.

1 Thessalonians 2:12 NASB

Therefore, since we have this ministry, as we have received mercy, we do not give up. Instead, we have renounced shameful secret things, not walking in deceit or distorting God's message, but in God's sight we commend ourselves to every person's conscience by an open display of the truth.

2 Corinthians 4:1-2 HCSB

We must not become tired of doing good. We will receive our harvest of eternal life at the right time if we do not give up.

Galatians 6:9 NCV

Blessed are those who hunger and thirst for righteousness, because they will be filled.

Matthew 5:6 HCSB

DOING THE RIGHT THING

The righteous one will live by his faith.

Habakkuk 2:4 HCSB

And the world is passing away, and the lust of it; but he who does the will of God abides forever.

1 John 2:17 NKJV

Because the eyes of the Lord are on the righteous and His ears are open to their request. But the face of the Lord is against those who do evil.

1 Peter 3:12 HCSB

Flee from youthful passions, and pursue righteousness, faith, love, and peace, along with those who call on the Lord from a pure heart.

2 Timothy 2:22 HCSB

Sow righteousness for yourselves and reap faithful love; break up your untilled ground. It is time to seek the Lord until He comes and sends righteousness on you like the rain.

Hosea 10:12 HCSB

PEACE

And the peace of God, which surpasses every thought, will guard your hearts and your minds in Christ Jesus. Finally brothers, whatever is true, whatever is honorable, whatever is just, whatever is pure, whatever is lovely, whatever is commendable—if there is any moral excellence and if there is any praise—dwell on these things.

Philippians 4:7-8 HCSB

Abundant peace belongs to those who love Your instruction; nothing makes them stumble.

Psalm 119:165 HCSB

You will keep in perfect peace him whose mind is steadfast, because he trusts in you.

Isaiah 26:3 NIV

I have told you these things so that in Me you may have peace. In the world you have suffering. But take courage! I have conquered the world.

John 16:33 HCSB

GOD'S GRACE

But God, who is abundant in mercy, because of His great love that He had for us, made us alive with the Messiah even though we were dead in trespasses. By grace you are saved!

Ephesians 2:4-5 HCSB

My grace is sufficient for you, for My strength is made perfect in weakness.

2 Corinthians 12:9 NKJV

And we have seen and testify that the Father has sent the Son as Savior of the world.

1 John 4:14 NKJV

For by grace you are saved through faith, and this is not from yourselves; it is God's gift—not from works, so that no one can boast.

Ephesians 2:8-9 HCSB

In Him we have redemption through His blood, the forgiveness of our trespasses, according to the riches of His grace that He lavished on us with all wisdom and understanding.

Ephesians 1:7-8 HCSB

BIBLE STUDY

All Scripture is inspired by God and is profitable for teaching, for rebuking, for correcting, for training in righteousness, so that the man of God may be complete, equipped for every good work.

2 Timothy 3:16-17 HCSB

Man shall not live by bread alone, but by every word that proceeds from the mouth of God.

Matthew 4:4 NKJV

Heaven and earth will pass away, but My words will never pass away.

Matthew 24:35 HCSB

For the word of God is living and effective and sharper than any two-edged sword, penetrating as far as to divide soul, spirit, joints, and marrow; it is a judge of the ideas and thoughts of the heart.

Hebrews 4:12 HCSB

THE DIRECTION OF YOUR THOUGHTS

Set your minds on what is above, not on what is on the earth.

Colossians 3:2 HCSB

Brothers, don't be childish in your thinking, but be infants in evil and adult in your thinking.

1 Corinthians 14:20 HCSB

Guard your heart above all else, for it is the source of life.

Proverbs 4:23 HCSB

May the words of my mouth and the meditation of my heart be acceptable to You, Lord, my rock and my Redeemer.

Psalm 19:14 HCSB

Commit your works to the Lord, and your thoughts will be established.

Proverbs 16:3 NKJV

TRUSTING GOD

Lord, I turn my hope to You. My God, I trust in You. Do not let me be disgraced; do not let my enemies gloat over me.

Psalm 25:1-2 HCSB

He granted their request because they trusted in Him.

1 Chronicles 5:20 HCSB

The one who understands a matter finds success, and the one who trusts in the Lord will be happy.

Proverbs 16:20 HCSB

The fear of man is a snare, but the one who trusts in the Lord is protected.

Proverbs 29:25 HCSB

Those who trust in the Lord are like Mount Zion. It cannot be shaken; it remains forever.

Psalm 125:1 HCSB

GOD'S FAITHFULNESS

I will sing of the tender mercies of the Lord forever! Young and old will hear of your faithfulness. Your unfailing love will last forever. Your faithfulness is as enduring as the heavens.

Psalm 89:1-2 NLT

God is faithful, by whom you were called into the fellowship of His Son, Jesus Christ our Lord.

1 Corinthians 1:9 NKJV

Because of the LORD'S great love we are not consumed, for his compassions never fail. They are new every morning; great is your faithfulness.

Lamentations 3:22-23 NIV

Blessed is he whose help is the God of Jacob, whose hope is in the LORD his God, the Maker of heaven and earth, the sea, and everything in them—the LORD, who remains faithful forever.

Psalm 146:5-6 NIV

PRAISE AND THANKSGIVING

It is good to give thanks to the Lord, and to sing praises to Your name, O Most High.

Psalm 92:1 NKJV

And let the peace of the Messiah, to which you were also called in one body, control your hearts. Be thankful.

Colossians 3:15 HCSB

Therefore as you have received Christ Jesus the Lord, walk in Him, rooted and built up in Him and established in the faith, just as you were taught, and overflowing with thankfulness.

Colossians 2:6-7 HCSB

In everything give thanks; for this is the will of God in Christ Jesus for you.

1 Thessalonians 5:18 NKJV

So that at the name of Jesus every knee should bow—of those who are in heaven and on earth and under the earth—and every tongue should confess that Jesus Christ is Lord, to the glory of God the Father.

Philippians 2:10-11 HCSB

JOY

Rejoice in the Lord always. I will say it again: Rejoice!

Philippians 4:4 HCSB

You will show me the way of life, granting me the joy of your presence and the pleasures of living with you forever.

Psalm 16:11 NLT

David and the whole house of Israel were celebrating before the Lord.

2 Samuel 6:5 HCSB

Their sorrow was turned into rejoicing and their mourning into a holiday. They were to be days of feasting, rejoicing, and of sending gifts to one another and the poor.

Esther 9:22 HCSB

At the dedication of the wall of Jerusalem, they sent for the Levites wherever they lived and brought them to Jerusalem to celebrate the joyous dedication with thanksgiving and singing accompanied by cymbals, harps, and lyres.

Nehemiah 12:27 HCSB

ABUNDANCE

I have come that they may have life, and that they may have it more abundantly.

John 10:10 NKJV

And God is able to make every grace overflow to you, so that in every way, always having everything you need, you may excel in every good work.

2 Corinthians 9:8 HCSB

Until now you have asked for nothing in My name. Ask and you will receive, that your joy may be complete.

John 16:24 HCSB

Come to terms with God and be at peace; in this way good will come to you.

Job 22:21 HCSB

My cup runs over. Surely goodness and mercy shall follow me all the days of my life; and I will dwell in the house of the Lord forever.

Psalm 23:5-6 NKJV

ANXIETY

Therefore don't worry about tomorrow, because tomorrow will worry about itself. Each day has enough trouble of its own.

Matthew 6:34 HCSB

Anxiety in a man's heart weighs it down, but a good word cheers it up.

Proverbs 12:25 HCSB

Why am I so depressed? Why this turmoil within me? Put your hope in God, for I will still praise Him, my Savior and my God.

Psalm 42:11 HCSB

In the multitude of my anxieties within me, Your comforts delight my soul.

Psalm 94:19 NKJV

Be anxious for nothing, but in everything by prayer and supplication, with thanksgiving, let your requests be made known to God.

Philippians 4:6 NKJV

CONFIDENCE

God also bound himself with an oath, so that those who received the promise could be perfectly sure that he would never change his mind. So God has given us both his promise and his oath. These two things are unchangeable because it is impossible for God to lie. Therefore, we who have fled to him for refuge can take new courage, for we can hold on to his promise with confidence.

Hebrews 6:17-18 NLT

The result of righteousness will be peace; the effect of righteousness will be quiet confidence forever.

Isaiah 32:17 HCSB

I've told you all this so that trusting me, you will be unshakable and assured, deeply at peace. In this godless world you will continue to experience difficulties. But take heart! I've conquered the world.

John 16:33 MSG

You are my hope; O Lord GOD, You are my confidence.

Psalm 71:5 NASB

ENCOURAGING OTHERS

I want their hearts to be encouraged and joined together in love,
so that they may have all the riches of assured understanding,
and have the knowledge of God's mystery—Christ.

Colossians 2:2 HCSB

And let us be concerned about one another in order to promote
love and good works.

Hebrews 10:24 HCSB

Carry one another's burdens; in this way you will fulfill the law
of Christ.

Galatians 6:2 HCSB

But encourage each other daily, while it is still called today, so
that none of you is hardened by sin's deception.

Hebrews 3:13 HCSB

Iron sharpens iron, and one man sharpens another.

Proverbs 27:17 HCSB

GOD'S COMMANDMENTS

If only you had paid attention to My commands. Then your peace would have been like a river, and your righteousness like the waves of the sea.

Isaiah 48:18 HCSB

This is how we are sure that we have come to know Him: by keeping His commands.

1 John 2:3 HCSB

For this is the love of God, that we keep His commandments. And His commandments are not burdensome.

1 John 5:3 NKJV

Follow the whole instruction the Lord your God has commanded you, so that you may live, prosper, and have a long life in the land you will possess.

Deuteronomy 5:33 HCSB

He who has My commandments and keeps them, it is he who loves Me. And he who loves Me will be loved by My Father, and I will love him and manifest Myself to him.

John 14:21 NKJV

GOD'S PRESENCE

Draw near to God, and He will draw near to you.

James 4:8 HCSB

You will seek Me and find Me when you search for Me with all your heart.

Jeremiah 29:13 HCSB

The Lord is near all who call out to Him, all who call out to Him with integrity. He fulfills the desires of those who fear Him; He hears their cry for help and saves them.

Psalm 145:18-19 HCSB

Surely goodness and mercy shall follow me all the days of my life: and I will dwell in the house of the Lord for ever.

Psalm 23:6 KJV

I am not alone, because the Father is with Me.

John 16:32 HCSB

GOD'S TIMING

He said to them, "It is not for you to know times or periods that the Father has set by His own authority."

Acts 1:7 HCSB

Therefore the Lord is waiting to show you mercy, and is rising up to show you compassion, for the Lord is a just God. Happy are all who wait patiently for Him.

Isaiah 30:18 HCSB

But those who wait on the LORD shall renew their strength; they shall mount up with wings like eagles, they shall run and not be weary, they shall walk and not faint.

Isaiah 40:31 NKJV

To everything there is a season, a time for every purpose under heaven.

Ecclesiastes 3:1 NKJV

I waited patiently for the LORD; and He inclined to me, and heard my cry.

Psalm 40:1 NKJV

JESUS

The next day John saw Jesus coming toward him and said, "Here is the Lamb of God, who takes away the sin of the world!"

John 1:29 HCSB

I am the door. If anyone enters by Me, he will be saved.

John 10:9 NKJV

I have come as a light into the world, so that everyone who believes in Me would not remain in darkness.

John 12:46 HCSB

I am the true vine, and My Father is the vineyard keeper. Every branch in Me that does not produce fruit He removes, and He prunes every branch that produces fruit so that it will produce more fruit.

John 15:1-2 HCSB

But we do see Jesus—made lower than the angels for a short time so that by God's grace He might taste death for everyone— crowned with glory and honor because of the suffering of death.

Hebrews 2:9 HCSB